Mexico's Middle Class in the Neoliberal Era

MEXICO'S MIDDLE CLASS
IN THE
NEOLIBERAL ERA

Dennis Gilbert

The University of Arizona Press

Tucson

The University of Arizona Press
© 2007 The Arizona Board of Regents

Library of Congress Cataloging-in-Publication Data

Gilbert, Dennis L.
Mexico's middle class in the neoliberal era / Dennis Gilbert.
p. cm.
Includes bibliographical references and index.
ISBN-13: 978-0-8165-2590-4 (hardcover : alk. paper)
ISBN-10: 0-8165-2590-0 (hardcover : alk. paper)
1. Middle class—Mexico. I. Title.
HT690.M4G54 2007
305.5'50972—dc22
2006026215

Manufactured in the United States of America on acid-free, archival-
quality paper containing a minimum of 50% post-consumer waste
and processed chlorine free.

12 11 10 09 08 07   6 5 4 3 2 1

CONTENTS

List of Illustrations   vii

Preface   ix

1   Introduction   3

2   Origins: The Growth Decades   23

3   From Growth to Neoliberalism   37

4   Magicians: Surviving the Crisis of the 1990s   45

5   The Middle Class and the Post-Revolutionary Regime   57

6   After Tlatelolco   73

7   The July 2000 Elections   84

8   Mixed Fortunes and Political Disaffection   93

Epilogue: The July 2006 Election   102

APPENDIX A. Descriptions of the Surveys   105

APPENDIX B. Cuernavaca and the Cuernavaca Sample   108

APPENDIX C. Notes on Defining and Measuring the Middle Class   113

Notes   119

Bibliographic Notes   125

Bibliography   129

Index   137

ILLUSTRATIONS

Photographs

1. Middle manager's home: front yard   7
2. Middle manager with his wife and son   7
3. Middle manager's home: master bedroom   7
4. Middle manager's home: dining room/kitchen   7
5. Professional with his wife   8
6. Professional's home: dining room   8
7. Professional's home: front yard/pool   8
8. Teacher with her husband   9
9. Teacher's home: dining room   9
10. Teacher's home: living room   9

Tables

1.1. Labor force comparisons   4
1.2. Class identification   15
1.3. Distribution of households by occupation and income   16
1.4. Material indicators   17
1.5. Education of family heads   18
1.6. Racial identification by class   19
2.1. Growth of the middle class, 1940–1980   29
2.2. Occupational mobility   31
4.1. Private school enrollment in Cuernavaca   49
5.1. Political attitudes in 1959   65
6.1. Some class differences in political culture, 2000   81
7.1. Party preference in presidential elections, by class   88

7.2. Within-class variation among middle-class voters, 2000   89

7.3. Between-class differences in vote for Fox in 2000   90

8.1. Middle-class households   95

8.2. Median monthly household income   96

8.3. Passenger car production for the domestic market   96

8.4. Material indicators, 1984–2000   97

8.5. Educational attainment: heads of households   99

8.6. Young adults (17–22) working 20 hours or more per week   99

8.7. Private school attendance of children ages 6–11 years   100

E.1. Party preference in 2006 presidential election   103

B.1. Economic profile of families   110

B.2. Social profile of families   111

C.1. Index of median earnings by occupation   116

C.2. Earnings of male heads by age and occupational category   116

My twin concerns in this book are the mixed fortunes and shifting politics of the Mexican middle class, especially during the last two decades, as Mexico has embraced a new, market-driven economic model and abandoned one-party rule. How big, I ask, is the middle class? How has it fared in Mexico's changing, often troubled economy? ("Falling, falling, falling," answers one of the disillusioned middle-class Mexicans interviewed by the *New York Times* [2002].) How important were disaffected middle-class voters in the defeat of the long-ruling Partido Revolucionario Institucional (PRI) in 2000?

In 1999, I began interviewing middle-class families in Cuernavaca, a midsized city about an hour from Mexico City. By 2005, I had talked to members of fifty-two families, in many cases multiple members of the same household. Some informants were interviewed repeatedly over a period of years. These interviews, lasting one to three hours, were far ranging. I asked about the economic situation of the household, family history, personal biography, and, as the 2000 elections approached, about politics. Many of my questions focused on middle-class "survival strategies" in periods of economic stress. I especially wanted to know how middle-class families had been affected by and responded to the economic crisis set off by the December 1994 monetary debacle known as the Peso Crisis. What economic losses had they suffered? How had they adjusted household spending? What resources —social, economic, or cultural—did they have to defend themselves?

My account of the middle class blends personal narratives with impersonal survey statistics. To place what I was learning in Cuernavaca in a broader context, I analyzed data from nearly a dozen national surveys. Successive waves of the government's periodic survey of household finances allowed me to trace the economic fortunes of middle-class families since the mid-1980s. Mexico data from Almond and Verba's classic 1959 Civic Culture study and recent World Values Surveys revealed middle-class political attitudes. To analyze the middle-class vote in the critical 2000 elections I relied on data from the *Reforma/Los Angles Times* exit poll. (When my own analysis of data from these surveys is the basis for statements made in the text, they are cited by title and the date they were conducted, as follows: Civic Culture-1959. See appendix A for further information on the surveys.)

The Cuernavaca interviews and the survey analyses proved to be, even more than I had anticipated, complementary sources. The surveys provided a national, statistically representative basis for generalizations about the Mexican middle class. The interviews, on the other hand, yielded a sense of the rich substance, variety, and meaning of personal experience, which is inevitably paved over by statistical generalization. What I heard in the interviews influenced my understanding (and sometimes skepticism) of survey categories. What the surveys revealed sometimes forced me to reread my interview notes and return to informants with more questions.

My narrative reaches back to the 1940s when the modern middle class emerged. After chapter 1, which takes up the knotty problem of defining middle class, chapters 2 and 3 trace the economic history of the middle class, from the postwar boom to the uncertain 1990s. Chapter 4 examines the survival strategies of middle-class families in the economic crisis of the mid-1990s. The next three chapters deal with the political evolution of the middle class, focusing on its changing relationship to the PRI and, finally, its pivotal role in the 2000 elections. Chapter 8 relates the political transformation of the middle class to its changing fortunes in the Neoliberal Era. The epilogue examines the role of the middle class in the July 2006 elections.

The appendices contain extensive information about the methodological bases of my research, including descriptions of the surveys, supplementary information about Cuernavaca and the Cuernavaca sample, and notes on the definition of middle class.

This book would never have seen the light of day without the support of many friends and colleagues. I am especially grateful to Fernando and Carmen Díez de Urdanivia, who opened their home to me, shared their rich knowledge of Mexican culture, and aided my research in a thousand practical ways. Claudio Stern, who encouraged this project from the beginning, was generous with his knowledge of the Mexican class system. Claudio, Lourdes Benería, Cynthia Mc-Clintock, Oscar Ruíz, and Henry Rutz gave me thoughtful readings of the papers from which the book evolved. Bill LeoGrande, Eric Van Young, Rod Camp, and Dan Chambliss read the complete manuscript and helped me to sharpen and clarify my own ideas. I am grateful to Nina Serafino, who took most of the photographs of middle-class homes in chapter 1. Alejandro Moreno and Susan Pinkus helped me gain access to two important data sets and provided good advice on their analysis. Robin Vanderwall skillfully prepared the manuscript for publication. Hamilton College, my institutional home, allowed me time to work on this project and financed my travel to Mexico. I am, finally, thankful to Trinity University in Washington and Bob Maguire, my host at Trinity, for providing the ideal setting for writing this book.

I've drawn on papers previously published in the *Journal of Latin American Anthropology* and *Estudios Sociológicos* (Gilbert 2005a, 2005b). This material is used here with the permission of the journals.

MEXICO'S MIDDLE CLASS
IN THE
NEOLIBERAL ERA

CHAPTER 1

Introduction

R̄oberto Marín,[1] a teacher who moved to Cuernavaca in 1960, found a "traditional, picturesque town of white walls and tile roofs." At the time, Cuernavaca had a population under 40,000 and was known to Mexicans as a tourist destination, where affluent families maintained second homes.

Marín had arrived at a moment of stability in the city's agitated twentieth-century history. Cuernavaca is the state capital of Morelos, once home to Emiliano Zapata's peasant rebellion and one of the most bitterly contested states during the violent years of the Mexican revolution. The upheaval destroyed the state's wealthy planter class. Cuernavaca was repeatedly besieged, occupied, ravaged, and abandoned by contending forces. For a time, the city was depopulated, with much of its depleted middle class fleeing to Mexico City. Not until 1940 did Cuernavaca regain its modest pre-revolutionary (1910) population.

The quiet town that Marín knew was transformed almost beyond recognition in the decades after his arrival. By the time I started interviewing middle-class families in Cuernavaca, the city had grown to nearly 700,000 inhabitants. Forty-two percent of all Cuernavacans were born elsewhere (INEGI 1997: 78). The local economy, once dependent on agriculture, now revolves around commerce, services, and manufacturing. An industrial park, established in the late 1960s, attracted multinational firms such as Nissan and Firestone. On weekday mornings, Cuernavaca's growing integration with nearby Mexico City is in evidence at Terminal de la Selva, the busy bus station that serves the sprawling middle-class neighborhoods to the north and west of the old city center. Between 6 and 11 a.m., forty-two buses depart for Mexico City, including ten deluxe-service "Golden Executive"

TABLE 1.1 Labor force comparisons
(percent of labor force)

Profession	Cuernavaca	Average 44 largest cities
Professional, technical, or managerial occupation	16.7	17.5
Government employee	6.1	5.8
Employer	6.1	5.0
Earnings more than 5× minimum wage	10.1	12.5

Source: INEGI 2000

buses. They are joined on the toll road to Mexico City by large numbers of private cars. Many of the travelers are daily commuters.

Evidence from the government's periodic survey of urban employment suggests that Cuernavaca has become, in economic terms, a typical Mexican city. The survey tracks the labor force in the forty-four "most important" urban areas, covering nearly all cities over 100,000 in population. Three-quarters of middle-class families, as I will define them, live in these cities. According to the survey, the distribution of Cuernavaca's labor force across economic sectors is close to the all-city average (table 1.1). The proportions of Cuernavacans who hold professional and managerial jobs, employ others, or have relatively high earnings are also close to national urban averages. These characteristics make Cuernavaca an ideal setting for a study of the Mexican middle class.[2]

This book places what I learned in Cuernavaca in historical and national context. Drawing on the interviews, my own analysis of national survey data,[3] and the work of other writers, it explores the modern history of the Mexican middle class, its growth, its shifting economic fortunes, and its political transformation.

Three Families

Among those I interviewed in Cuernavaca were the three couples pictured in front of their homes on the adjoining pages. The first, a midlevel manager and his wife, were photographed with their thirteen-year-old son. The manager was born to a peasant family, trained as an accountant, and is now employed by a national corporation. He earns 16,000 pesos a month (about $1,600 U.S. at the current rate of exchange, but worth more than that in Mexico). Despite her secretarial skills, his wife does not work outside the home. Their son attends an expensive private school. True to his profession, the manager carefully tracks and controls household expenses, refusing, for example, to allow his wife to hire a maid. The three live in a well-constructed, thoughtfully furnished, 1,700-square-foot home with three bedrooms and two and a half baths, in a pleasant middle-class neighborhood. They own two cars: a relatively new Volkswagen Jetta and an older subcompact. The family recently returned from a short vacation in Acapulco.

The second couple, an independent professional and his wife, is accustomed to an income that is at least twice the first family's. But the economic crisis of the 1990s has sharply reduced his earnings. She manages a professional building they own. Their three children, now in their twenties and thirties and married, attended costly private schools and private universities. The couple's expensively furnished home, in an upscale neighborhood, is over 5,000 square feet, with four bedrooms and three and a half baths. The house is graced by a well-tended garden, surrounding a small pool. Like the first family, the couple owns two cars, including a two-year-old Chevrolet Impala. They are planning a trip to Spain.

The third couple, a public school teacher and her husband, retired with a pension from PEMEX, the state oil monopoly, has a combined income of about 6,000 pesos a month. They have three college-age children, who attended public schools and are currently enrolled in public universities. Their home is about the size of the first family's, with three bedrooms and two baths, but it is of cheaper construction and located in a less appealing middle-class neighborhood, far from the center of the city. In their dining room, a new washing machine waits to be uncrated and installed. Computer gear is visible in the living room. (The two other families also have computers, but they are not kept in places where they would be noticed by a casual visitor.) The family owns a single, older car and spends little on leisure. The teacher recently returned from a visit to her sister in nearby Mexico City.

Though these three families differ in obvious ways, they have much in common that sets them apart from the popular majority. They own good-sized homes, built of substantial materials.[4] They have telephones, computers, and automobiles. They expect their children to attend college. I consider them all middle class, but I should explain why.

Who's Middle Class?

Middle class has long been regarded as a problematic social category resistant to any serious attempt at definition. Karl Marx puzzled over bourgeois society's growing "horde of flunkeys, the soldiers, sailors, police, lower officials . . . mistresses, grooms, clowns and jugglers . . . ill-paid artists, musicians, lawyers, physicians, scholars, schoolmasters and inventors, etc." (Marx 1963: I, 573). His writings are replete with vaguely defined references to middle classes, middle bourgeoisie, intermediate strata and the like.[5] Since Marx, generations of scholars, in Mexico as elsewhere, have debated whether the diverse population typically lumped into the middle class is really a class at all or just an incoherent residual category.

In a 1955 article on "The Middle Class in Mexico," sociologist Lucio Mendieta Nuñez confesses that he has no idea how to delineate his topic: "[It] seems to us impossible to define the middle class" (Mendieta Nuñez 1955: 521). In her book on the politics of the Mexican middle class, Soledad Loaeza observes, "The notion of middle class is almost always accompanied by some adjective: upper, lower, emerging, revolutionary, progressive, conservative." Her comment suggests the concept is too weak to stand alone. "From numerous studies that somehow mention it in any form, the general impression is that of a blurry photograph whose meaning depends on who is looking at it" (Loaeza 1988: 11).

Photographs: Three middle-class homes. *1–4:* a middle manager's home, with views of the dining room/kitchen and master bedroom. *5–7:* an independent professional's home, including views of the dining room and enclosed front yard with pool. *8–10:* a teacher's home—note the new washing machine, still in its crate, in the dining room, and the computer gear in the living room.

1

2

3

4

5

6

7

8

9

10

In remarks prepared for a 1975 party conference on the middle class, PRI leader Jesús Reyes Heroles also seems defeated by the problem of definition. Reyes Heroles, a respected intellectual, tries and discards various criteria that might be used. Non-manual work? Income? Lifestyle? Self-employment? Durable consumer goods? All seem inadequate. Even the term "middle class" seems wrong. Reyes Heroles insists on referring to the "middle classes," a usage favored by writers who wish to emphasize the heterogeneity of the middle-class groups (Reyes Heroles 1988). In 1975, such matters were, as we will see in chapter 6, of more than academic interest for a PRI leadership increasingly anxious about middle-class political loyalties.

For Marx and his intellectual heirs, the growing middle sectors, however labeled and defined, present a triple challenge: (1) *They should not exist at all or at least should not be growing.* Marx described two fundamental classes in capitalist societies, the bourgeoisie and the proletariat, whose interactions control the dynamics of such societies. At first he suggested that intermediate classes exist as atavistic survivals, but are likely to disappear. Later, he plainly acknowledged their steady expansion in capitalist societies (Marx 1963: II, 573), but he never found a place for them in his theory of capitalist development. (2) *They do not constitute a class.* The fundamental social classes are defined by their reciprocal relationship to the means of production— as owners or as unpropertied workers compelled to sell their labor to the owners. But independent professionals, government workers, shop owners,[6] teachers, and many others who might be considered middle class have no obvious or shared relationship to the means of production. (3) *They have no common basis for class consciousness.* Without shared economic interests to unite them, they are unlikely to evolve a sense of themselves as a class, with interests to defend in opposition to other classes. Can we, for example, really expect the three couples described above to develop a common political perspective?

Marxist writers have strained to close this gap between empirical reality and orthodox theory with formulations emphasizing the quasi-bourgeois or quasi-proletarian character of middle-sector positions. Ranking corporate executives, theorists suggest, share the interests of the owners of capital. Low-level office workers are being "proletarianized" by slim wages and routinized work that bring them close to the experience of factory workers. Midlevel managers are occupants of "contradictory" class locations, since they are at once bosses and wage workers.

Contemporary conceptions of the middle class often reflect the influence of the German sociologist Max Weber.[7] Writing a generation after Marx, Weber avoided some of the theoretical traps that have stymied Marxist analyses of modern class structures. He was not wedded to a dichotomous conception of class structure and made no assumptions about class consciousness. For Weber as for Marx, class was an economic distinction, but Weber understood class position broadly as market situation rather than specifically as relationship to the means of production. The lives of the members of a Weberian class are shaped by shared advantages or disadvantages in labor, capital, or commercial markets. Weber's conception of class highlights two variables that receive limited emphasis in Marx: occupation and income. Occupation is obviously a key determinant of market situation in modern societies. (The well-trained engineer, for example, has a market advantage invisible from Marx's vantage point.) Income is the clearest measure of market value.

We could conceive of a Weberian middle class as consisting of people with certain kinds of occupations. But which occupations would qualify and why? We might define middle-class jobs by educational requirements, by income level, by authority over others, or autonomy at work. All these have been used by researchers, sometimes in ways that seem rather arbitrary, to define social classes. Weber provides no guidance. He tells us that occupation (like property) is an important class variable, but cannot say how or where to draw class boundaries around groups of occupations. Given the diversity of the usual candidates for inclusion in the middle class, this is no small problem.

It is worth noting that the concept of middle class is less problematic for most Mexicans than it is for most theorists, national or foreign—perhaps because of the relatively small size of Mexico's middle class and the wide material gulf that separates it from the mass of the population. While scholars struggle with class boundaries, Mexicans have no difficulty naming middle-class neighborhoods, middle-class stores, or middle-class jobs and middle-class incomes.

A Working Definition

My own approach to class in this book has been influenced by Marx and Weber and by the tradition of empirical studies of the Mexican class structure based on national occupation and income data.[8] I have assumed that there is no one correct answer to questions about how to define classes or where, precisely, to draw their boundaries. The social reality to which class refers is too complex and too inconsistent, and our purposes as students of that reality are too varied, for that kind of finality. There are, however, answers that are useful and illuminating.

I have made two other assumptions. One is that households, rather than individuals, should be considered the basic units of classes, since the members of a household live under the same roof, pool their resources, and share a common economic fate. (This is not to deny that economic inequalities may exist within households, based, for example, on gender.) For the purposes of this research, people are assigned to classes based on household characteristics. The other assumption, especially relevant to a study of the middle class, is that living standards should be understood in relative rather than absolute terms. As recently as 1960, the majority of Mexican homes consisted of one room, and only a third had running water inside. At the time, sociologist Pablo Gonzalez Casanova (1968: 66–67) included in his definition of the middle class a home with three or more rooms and running water. Today one-room homes are rare, three rooms are common, and almost two-thirds of Mexican homes have running water (ENIGH-2000). Absolute standards inevitably become obsolete as incomes rise.

I conceive of the Mexican middle class as consisting of *families headed by individuals with non-routine, non-manual occupations, living on incomes comfortably above the popular average but below the peak of the national pyramid.* I particularly have in mind independent and salaried professionals, managers, teachers, technicians, bureaucrats, and merchants (but not low-level office workers or retail clerks), with household *incomes at least 50 percent higher than the median household income.*

This approach defines middle class in terms of the character of occupations and family living standards. The occupations singled out allow people greater autonomy and require them to exercise greater discretion on the job. The work is not repetitive or closely supervised (in contrast, for example, to the work of an assembly line worker or low-level office worker). Many involve the exercise of authority over others. They require relatively high levels of knowledge or training, ranging from the physician's formal preparation for his profession to the merchant's cumulative understanding of his market and the financial aspects of his enterprise. These jobs are also relatively well paid and offer earnings that rise significantly over the course of a career (see appendix C for details).

The defining middle-class income—50 percent higher than the household median—is, of course, a relative standard that will vary over time with changes in national living standards. Aside from its explicit purpose of incorporating a contemporary standard of living into the conception of middle class, the income floor has an additional practical advantage. It reduces the distortion introduced by overly broad occupational categories. A term such as *comerciantes* may, for example, cover substantial merchants and others who are one step above street peddlers. The income standard tends to filter out the latter.[9]

The proposed income threshold is, by design, well above the Mexican average. But it is modest by international middle-class standards. In 2000, 150 percent of the median monthly household income was a little less than 6,000 pesos or about $600 U.S. at the current exchange rate (which conveniently remained around 10 pesos to the dollar during the research period).[10] But the real purchasing power of Mexican households at this income level was, according to a careful estimate, closer to $900 U.S.—still a modest monthly income.[11]

Household budgets collected from some of the families interviewed suggest that 6,000 pesos would probably be (just) sufficient to cover middle-class essentials such as decent housing, a telephone, and an automobile, along with other, basic household expenses. A middling middle-class budget of 15,000 pesos would allow for greater comfort and such luxuries as private schools, a second car, some domestic help and an annual vacation. A relatively high middle-class budget of 30,000 or 40,000 pesos would cover a deluxe version of the middling budget, with some room for travel abroad. The teacher, manager, and independent professional pictured earlier exemplify these living standards.

I have specified an income floor, but not set a precise income ceiling for the middle class. The reason is that the stratum of wealthy investors, heirs, ranking executives, top professionals, and highly successful small-business owners who might reasonably be labeled capitalist class or upper class is simply too small to matter in even the largest of national surveys. The rough consensus of my informants in Cuernavaca would place the upper limit for middle class at 65,000 pesos per month—not quite enough to permit a family to check into a five-star hotel or plan a few weeks in Italy without carefully considering the expense involved. Only a small fraction of a percent of Mexican families have incomes above 65,000, according to the national household survey analyzed in the next section. Even the proportion of households with monthly incomes above 50,000 was under 1 percent in 2000. Incomes in excess of 35,000 were rare among my Cuernavaca informants.

When defining the middle-class with national survey data, therefore, I will not impose an upper income limit. The people I will be describing with such data might, more accurately be labeled "the privileged classes," but, as a practical matter, it seemed more reasonable to simply label them middle class, as 99 percent of them certainly are.

Do the people I am calling middle class think of themselves as middle class? My Cuernavaca informants seemed to, though I never asked directly. There is some national evidence on this question. In 2000, the World Values Survey asked Mexicans which of five classes they belonged to. Eighty-five percent of middle-class respondents (as defined here) described themselves as upper or lower middle class; a significant minority of non-middle-class respondents identified themselves as lower middle class (table 1.2).[12] I should emphasize here that my own approach is not based on self-placement or public perceptions of the class order but on the character of work and standard of living.

A final note on class labels: as a matter of convenience, I will usually refer to the diverse population of households that do not qualify as middle class as the popular majority or the popular classes.

TABLE 1.2   Class identification (in percent)

Class self-identification	Respondent's class, based on occupation and income	
	Middle	Other
Upper	3	1
Upper middle	47	13
Lower middle	38	37
Working	5	16
Lower	5	24
Don't know	3	9
Total	100	100
N	(185)	(912)

Source: Author's analysis of WVS-2000 data
Note: Percentages have been rounded and may not total exactly 100.

A more nuanced analysis would certainly divide this large population into smaller, more coherent classes. The rural poor need to be distinguished from the more comfortable urban popular sectors. Families with upper-white-collar jobs, but less than middle-class incomes might be labeled the transitional class, since they approach middle-class levels in areas such as education and may well have middle-class backgrounds and middle-class ambitions. But my focus is on the middle class as defined in this chapter, which I will be comparing with all other households taken together.

A Statistical Portrait

Defined as suggested here, the middle class is not big—about one in five Mexican households. And it is certainly not located in the middle of the class structure. In Mexico, as in other countries characterized by mass poverty, the middle class is not average (as in the United States), but intermediate, sandwiched between the poor majority and the rich minority at the top. Mexicans, quite reasonably, think of the middle class as quasi-elite. Though restrictively defined, this middle class, as we have already seen, encompasses a wide range of living standards.

TABLE 1.3   Distribution of households by occupation and income
(percent of all households)

Multiples of median household income	Upper white collar	Other
Above 3.0	*10.6*	2.9
1.5–3.0	*8.9*	12.3
1.0–1.5	4.5	14.1
Under 1.0	5.4	41.2

Source: Author's analysis of ENIGH-2000 data

I have estimated the size of the middle class using year 2000 data from the Encuesta Nacional de Ingresos y Gastos de los Hogares (ENIGH), the Mexican government's large-scale (about 10,000 households), periodic survey of household finances. For conceptual and methodological simplicity, the analysis was limited to family households with heads under sixty-five. A family was considered middle class if the occupation of the household head fell into one of the non-routine white-collar categories and household income exceeded 150 percent of the ENIGH median in 2000.[13] By this standard, 19.5 percent of Mexican households are middle class.[14]

The distribution of Mexican families among occupational and income levels in 2000 is given in table 1.3. Occupations are split between the non-routine "upper white collar" jobs and all "others." Incomes are specified in multiples of the household median. For example, 10.6 percent of all families had incomes in excess of three times the median (about 11,500 pesos in 2000) and heads with upper-white-collar occupations. The 10.6 and 8.9 figures represent the middle class. The figures in bold print refer to the middle class.

The middle class captured with the ENIGH data is a relatively small, highly educated, distinctly privileged population, concentrated in larger cities and more prosperous regions of the country. Even the less affluent middle-class families enjoy a material standard that sets them apart from the popular majority. Their automobiles, telephones, and substantial homes fundamentally affect the character of everyday life. Although Mexicans at lower class levels may have access to such items, they are unlikely to possess them in combination, as middle-class families commonly do. Table 1.4 shows ownership rates for these relative luxuries across the same income and occupational categories used in the preceding table. Again, the middle-class categories are in bold print.

What is remarkable here is not the expected gap between the middle class and the impoverished majority but the sharp differences between middle-class families and other families at similar income levels. For example, 67 percent of middle-class families with incomes between 1.5 and 3.0 times the national median have ample, modern homes, compared with 48 percent of other families at this relatively high income level. These disparities suggest that middle-class families have social and economic advantages not revealed by current income. Middle-class families are, for example, more likely to have relatively affluent kin who might help a young couple buy a home. Their homes and cars represent accumulated wealth and are indicative of a superior capacity to *sustain* high levels of income and savings.

Middle-class privilege rests in part on superior education. Table 1.5 reveals the educational chasm separating the middle class from the popular majority. As we will observe in later chapters, middle-class families have been willing to make significant sacrifices to maintain this advantage. Their children are increasingly attending private schools. And the class disparities in education have been growing among younger Mexicans.

TABLE 1.4   Material indicators (percent of households with item)

Multiples of median household income	Telephone		Comfortable housing		Vehicle	
	Upper white collar	Other	Upper white collar	Other	Upper white collar	Other
Over 3.0	**92**	78	**89**	62	**90**	68
1.5–3.0	**71**	57	**67**	48	**67**	46
1.0–1.5	52	34	61	38	48	31
Under 1.0	37	13	35	13	20	12

Source: Author's analysis of ENIGH-2000 data
Note: Comfortable housing defined as residence with at least 5 rooms (including kitchen and bathroom) and modern plumbing, including flush toilet and hot water.

TABLE 1.5 Education of family heads
(minimum education completed, in percent)

Education level	Middle class	Popular
Primary (0–6 years)	17.4	60.4
Secondary/Preparatory	28.5	34.5
University (1+ years)	54.1	5.3
Total	100.0	100.0
N	(1,584)	(6,361)

Source: Author's analysis of ENIGH 2000 data
Note: Percentages have been rounded and may not total exactly 100.

The heads of middle-class families are most typically managers, professionals, teachers, and merchants. Two-thirds are salaried employees. By and large, they are concentrated in the tertiary sectors of the economy, such as commerce, health care, and education. Few work in government offices (7 percent), though many are publicly employed teachers or health professionals.

Only 12 percent of middle-class households are headed by women —in almost all cases single women—according to ENIGH data.[15] The income gap between male-headed and female-headed households is especially large for middle-class families. About half of middle-class wives are employed, providing, on average, about 25 percent of family income.

The middle class is, predictably, concentrated in the economically dynamic northern and central regions of the country. The states contiguous with the U.S. border are home to one in four middle-class families. At the other end of the country, the string of seven impoverished states stretching from Guerrero to Yucatan, with a larger population than the northern tier, account for just one in ten middle-class families. It is apparent (though ENIGH data do not permit precision here) that the largest concentration of middle-class households is in the region encompassing Mexico City, the contiguous parts of surrounding Mexico state and nearby cities such as Cuernavaca, which, in recent years, have been drawn into the economic orbit of the national capital.

The middle class is disproportionately urban in a highly urbanized nation. Seventy-five percent of middle-class families live in cities over 100,000—about 60 percent in the metropolitan areas, where only 35 percent of popular-class families live.[16] It makes little sense to speak of a rural middle class in contemporary Mexico, since less than 5 percent of middle-class families live in rural settings (under 2,500 population) and only 2 percent depend on agriculture.

A number of local studies point to another important aspect of the geography of class in Mexico: middle-class Mexicans live in increasing isolation from their compatriots. A characteristic of Mexican cities, observable in Cuernavaca, is the proliferation of middle-class neighborhoods and gated communities. Middle-class Mexicans shop in malls and supermarkets that cater to middle-class needs. These segregating tendencies are reinforced by an increasing dependence on private schools.[17]

The ENIGH data have nothing to say about race or ethnicity, but the 2000 World Values Survey asked interviewers in Mexico to classify respondents as *blanco, moreno claro, moreno oscuro, negro, indígena,* or *otro* (white, light brown, dark brown, black, indigenous, or other). The results, analyzed in table 1.6, confirm what is obvious to a casual observer of Mexican neighborhoods or workplaces: there is a rough correlation between class and color in Mexico. The Mexican middle class, at least to Mexican eyes, is diverse, but skewed to the lighter end of the racial spectrum.[18]

TABLE 1.6   Racial identification by class (in percent)

Race	Middle class	Popular
Blanco	27	14
Moreno claro	52	40
Moreno oscuro	19	43
Negro	*	*
Indígena	1	2
Other	1	1
Total	100	100
N	(182)	(890)

Source: Author's analysis of WVS-2000 data
*Less than 0.5

Family Fortunes and Political Change

The story I want to tell in this book concerns the shifting fortunes and political transformation of the Mexican middle class, especially in the last two decades of the twentieth century. The early chapters will not come as news to those who know Mexico. The modern middle class emerged in the period from 1940 to 1982, years of spectacular economic growth often referred to as "the Mexican miracle." In this period, the country's modernizing economy, swelling cities, and expanding education system created unprecedented opportunities for social mobility. Many of the middle-class people I interviewed in Cuernavaca grew up during this era in families of modest, in some cases impoverished, means. These years created a bond between the middle class and the PRI, Mexico's ruling party. Middle-class Mexicans, like their compatriots, had few illusions about the nation's corrupt, PRI-dominated political institutions. But they credited the party with bringing peace and social progress out of the chaos of the Mexican revolution and with setting in motion the economic model to which they owed their own good fortune.

Three critical moments shaped the subsequent history of the middle class:

August 1982—a financial crisis signaled the collapse of the miracle economy.

December 1994—another financial debacle, the so-called Peso Crisis, undermined middle-class faith in the regime.

July 2000—the middle class decisively rejected the ruling party in national elections.

In August 1982 the Mexican government jolted international markets with the announcement that the country would not be able to continue payments on its enormous international debt. The crisis had enduring consequences for Mexico. The economy fell into a deep recession that faded into a decade of stagnation. The country's rulers were compelled to abandon the inwardly oriented developmentalist policies that had guided the economy for the past four decades. Mexico adopted a neoliberal model that sharply reduced the government's role in the domestic economy and opened the country to the global market.

In the late 1980s and early 1990s, the middle class actually prospered in the new economy. Successive ENIGH surveys reveal steadily rising middle-class incomes. Middle-class Cuernavacans recall this period fondly. For many, there were big new cars, vacations abroad, and private schools for the kids. It was, remembers a physician in private practice, "my golden age." In the early 1990s, middle-class Mexicans had good reasons for their warm feelings toward President Carlos Salinas (1988–1994), the man most closely identified with the neoliberal model, whom they would later come to despise.

The Peso Crisis exploded in late December, days after Salinas left office. In 1995, the Mexican economy endured its worst contraction since the Great Depression. Middle-class households suffered a fall in income so abrupt and steep that I describe it as an income shock. Chapters 3 and 4 examine in some detail the economic damage inflicted on middle-class families in Cuernavaca and their responses to it. To defend a middle-class standard of living for themselves and the next generation, families drew on their own accumulated assets and the support of kin. Under financial stress, many were forced to make hard and revealing choices about their own priorities. Even those who escaped more or less unscathed emerged from the experience furious at a regime they had long supported.

In the late 1990s, middle-class households gradually regained most of the economic ground they lost in the wake of the Peso Crisis. There is ample evidence that the Mexican middle class at the end of the century was bigger and a good deal richer than it had been in the mid-1980s, when the country began its shift toward a neoliberal economic model. But the political consequences of the 1994–95 crisis proved more enduring than the economic damage.

The cumulative effect of a series of political, economic, and natural disasters since the late 1960s had already eroded middle-class support for the regime. In October 1968, a pro-democracy protest movement led by middle-class university students ended in the bloody Tlatelolco massacre. What most middle-class Mexicans thought about this event at the time is difficult to determine, but the Cuernavaca interviews show that it left its mark on the generation that had grown up in the prosperity of the miracle years and was occupying positions of influence by the 1990s.

Financial crises in 1976 and 1982, attributable to reckless economic policies; the government's shameful response to the 1985 Mexico City earthquake (which particularly affected middle-class neighborhoods); and its brazen manipulation of the vote count in the 1988 presidential election all contributed to growing middle-class disaffection. These events were interpreted through the lens of a middle-class political culture that was becoming more engaged, critical, and democratic and more open to change. But it took the Peso Crisis and the subsequent income shock to finally tear the middle class from its traditional political moorings. In 2000, the middle-class voters favored the presidential candidate of the opposition PAN party (*Partido Acción Nacional*) over the PRI candidate by 32 percent—a margin so lopsided that it may have been decisive in the defeat of the party that had ruled Mexico for most of the twentieth century.

CHAPTER 2

Origins

The Growth Decades

In the 1940s, Florencio Muñoz had a job he cherished, introducing Mexicans to Coca-Cola. He would drive to small towns where there was no electricity and few people had ever seen a motion picture, carrying a projector and a generator to show films featuring the Mexican comedian Cantinflas or "marvels of the world" travelogues. The screenings were organized as community events: a peso bought admission and a Coca-Cola, with seventy centavos going to the school (or *ejido* or hospital) where the event was held. Away from his home in Mexico City for two months at a time, Muñoz loved traveling, seeing new places, and, especially, meeting people. To make the right sort of impression, he dressed well and drove a late-model, carefully tended, company car. The job made him feel prosperous.

Julio Bernal was born during this period in an isolated village of 500 people. When he was six, the Bernals moved to Cuernavaca, where his father found a minimum wage job. The family's gradually improving fortunes and the expanding system of public education offered Julio possibilities his peasant grandparents could not have imagined. Ambitious, Julio made his way through *preparatoria* at state schools in Cuernavaca and in 1969 entered the medical school at National Autonomous University (UNAM) in Mexico City.

A generation apart, in their different ways, Julio Bernal and Florencio Muñoz took advantage of the opportunities offered by Mexico's transformation between 1940 and 1980. In 1940, Mexico was largely illiterate, rural, and heavily dependent on subsistence agriculture. Average life expectancy was about forty-one years (Prawda 1987: 84). The backward towns that Muñoz introduced to motion pictures and Coca-Cola in the 1940s were typical of the places Mexicans lived. A rapidly expanding, but still limited, highway system left much of the country beyond the reach of Muñoz's automobile. Where roads existed, he had to share them with peasants on foot, often carrying heavy bundles, and their animals. But by 1980, most Mexicans lived in cities, worked at urban occupations, and had at least five years of schooling. The national economy was eleven times larger than it had been in 1940 and real GNP per capita had almost quadrupled (Garza 2003: 26, 30; Oliveira and Roberts 1998: 311). In this dynamic environment, Mexico's embryonic middle class would flourish.

There had always been, even in colonial times, a thin stratum of Mexicans who could be considered middle class because they were neither rich nor poor but probably literate—minor officials, clerks, teachers, military officers, independent professionals, shopkeepers, small landowners, and others. At end of the nineteenth century, during the long reign of Porfirio Díaz, distinctively middle-class neighborhoods began to appear in Mexico City. Diaz himself told an American reporter in 1907 that Mexico had developed a middle class, which he described as the key to the county's future progress (Iturriaga 1951: 65–66). But nationally, this middle class remained small. More important, it did not seem to be growing in the last decade of the dictatorship (Hansen 1971: 22, 39). Perhaps the very character of Porfirian economic growth—defined by commodity exports, foreign investment, and a growing mass of debt peons in the countryside—was inimical to the sustained expansion of the middle class. Whatever potential it had was cut off by the violent disruption of the 1910 revolution.

Relative stability returned in the mid-1920s. The country entered an era of reconstruction and sometimes radical reform that laid a foundation for middle-class expansion after 1940. The economy grew little in this period that encompassed the Great Depression. Resources were being channeled into public education, mainly at the primary level, highway construction, and large-scale rural irrigation projects. In the late 1930s, a sweeping agrarian reform was carried out, breaking up large haciendas, eradicating debt peonage, distributing land to rural communities, and winning the loyalty of much of the peasantry for the new political regime. These programs and the related expansion of the state provided ample new opportunities for middle-class employment.

Three Growth Factors

The years from 1940 to 1982 define the period I refer to as the Growth Era, in contrast to the Neoliberal Era that followed. During these years, Mexico's economy and population expanded at unprecedented rates. The development of the middle class was favored by three factors: (1) the growth and diversification of the economy, (2) the urbanization of the population, and (3) the expansion of post-primary public education.

Economic Growth

Between 1940 and 1982, the Mexican economy grew, almost continuously, at annual rates in excess of 6 percent, a happy phenomenon often referred to as "the Mexican miracle."[1] Although growth slowed briefly in the mid-1970s, suggesting flaws in the economic model, it was soon restored. With the economy expanding at a pace well in excess of the country's high population growth rates, Mexicans at all levels were able to enjoy an improving standard of living. The benefits of prosperity, however, flowed disproportionately to the upper end of the income distribution. For example, from 1950 to 1969, the real incomes of the (typically middle-class) households in the top three deciles doubled, while the incomes of the bottom three rose about 40 percent (Hewitt de Alcántara 1977: 30).

During this period, Mexicans, especially among the elites that led the country, placed their faith in a set of economic policies that can be described as "developmentalist." They believed that it was the job of the state to promote economic development and growth by active intervention in the economy. Economic policy revolved around what was known as import substitution industrialization—literally, the promotion of industrial production for domestic markets traditionally supplied by imported goods. Backed by generous public financing, protective trade policies, and direct foreign investment in Mexican industry, the policy was extraordinarily successful. The value of manufactures tripled between 1940 and 1960, and quadrupled in the next twenty years (Garza 2003: 28). An important secondary focus of development policy was the expansion of large-scale commercial agriculture through the irrigation projects referred to earlier.

Despite the emphasis on manufacturing and commercial agriculture, the transformed Mexican economy would be dominated by its tertiary sector (by definition, commerce, transportation, and services, such as health, education, and finance). By 1980, the tertiary sector accounted for two-thirds of GNP and was on the verge of surpassing the primary sector (largely agriculture) in its share of total employment (Garza 2003: 26; INEGI 2001b: 197). The expansion of the tertiary sector was crucial for the growth of the middle class because it was (and is) the generator of most middle-class employment, including jobs for millions of teachers, lawyers, physicians, government bureaucrats, managers, and merchants.[2]

Urbanization

The middle class is predominantly an urban class. Even in 1940, when the national population was largely rural, the middle class was, by one careful estimate, 76 percent urban (Iturriaga 1951: 28). Rapid urbanization during the Growth Decades created ample opportunities for expansion of the middle class. In 1940 only 20 percent of Mexicans lived in urban places over 15,000 in population; by 1980, 55 percent did—nearly all in cities over 100,000. The biggest population flows were directed to the emerging industrial centers, especially Mexico City and Monterrey. By 1980, Mexico City had absorbed 13 million people, a large chunk of the national population. Other poles of urban growth were the northern border cities, such as Juárez, energized by expanding commerce with the United States, and cities like Hermosillo that profited from the growth of large-scale commercial agriculture in the surrounding countryside (Garza 2003: 41–46). The middle class thrived in these centers of economic and demographic dynamism.

What explains the colossal growth of cities during this period? An obvious factor is the general growth of the population, which was expanding at the highest rates in Mexican history. In the first forty years of the twentieth century, the population grew 44 percent.

In the next forty, it more than tripled (Garza 2003: 30–32). Birth rates were highest in the countryside. Even with the redistribution of land under the agrarian reform and massive investment in irriga- tion projects (concentrated, as it turned out, in the underpopulated north), Mexico's rural economy simply could not support the in- creased population. There were, however, jobs to be had in the cities, especially the industrializing cities. The same expanding transporta- tion system that brought the products and influences of the city to the countryside drew a migratory rush in the opposite direction. Middle- class and aspiring middle-class Mexicans moved, often from small towns to large cities, in search of benefits the city could provide: white-collar employment, superior educational opportunities, and such urban amenities as comfortable housing, health care, and varied entertainment.

Education

Howard Cline, a keen observer of Mexico during the Growth De- cades, wrote in 1960 that faith in education as a key to national progress had "become so fixed a dogma in today's Mexico that no one really questions it." Businessmen, Cline found, believed that educa- tion would create the productive labor force and the ardent con- sumers that a growing economy required. The middle class "wor- shiped" education, and to those on the lower margins of the middle class education was "a magic passport for social mobility" (Cline 1962: 191).

The urban economy with its expanding government and corpo- rate bureaucracies and its reliance on modern technologies had a voracious need for educated white-collar workers. Early on, a little education went a long way. In 1960, only 8 percent of the labor force had schooling beyond the primary level. At the time, fewer than half of the middle-class adults interviewed for a national survey had more than six years of schooling (Civic Culture-1959).[3] The gap between the demand for and supply of educated workers was decidedly to their advantage. Under these circumstances, a migrant to the big city from the provinces with a couple of years of secondary school and middle-class aspirations could expect to do quite well.

After 1960, renewed emphasis was placed on education, especially

post-primary education. In the space of two decades, overall spending on education tripled as a proportion of GNP, secondary school
enrollments climbed from 11 to 51 percent of twelve- to seventeen-
year-olds, and university enrollments rose from less than 3 to more
than 10 percent of college-age youth (Fuentes Molinar 1991: 231;
Dettmer and Loyo 1977: 256; Merrick 1998: 40; Marum Espinosa
1997: 260).

The expansion of the education system opened the middle class
to the future doctor Julio Bernal and many of his peers. But over time,
growth also contributed to a process of credential inflation and, according to some observers, a decline in the quality of public schools.
By 1980, a secondary education meant much less than it once had
in the job market, and a university degree no longer guaranteed
a professional-level job. Middle-class and aspiring middle-class families pushed their children to ever higher levels of education and
sought additional advantage, when they could afford it, by enrolling
them in private schools and universities (Lorey 1993). Nonetheless,
90 percent of students at all levels were still served by public institutions in 1980 (Secretaria de Educación Pública Web site).

Growth of the Middle Class

It was obvious to contemporaries that the interlocking expansions of
the economy, the cities, and the education system were producing a
rapid enlargement of the middle class. But just how big was the
middle class at the beginning and end of the Growth Era? A widely
cited series of estimates produced for the *Statistical Abstract of Latin
America* (SALA) and drawing on the pioneering work of José Iturriaga (1951) suggests that the middle class swelled from 16 to 33 percent of the population in the course of four decades (table 2.1). However, the SALA series is based on a liberal definition of middle class
that encompasses all white-collar workers, however menial their employment. This conception probably made more sense in the period
from 1895 to 1940 that is Iturriaga's focus—a time when literacy was
far from universal and low-level white-collar jobs were relatively well
paid—than it would after 1940.[4]

A better measure of middle-class growth is the count of people in
"higher non-manual" occupations compiled from census statistics by

TABLE 2.1   Growth of the middle class, 1940–1980
(middle class as percent of population)

Series	1940	1960	1980
Iturriaga/SALA	15.9	21.0	33.0
Oliveira, Roberts	4.5	9.4	13.4

Sources: First series, Iturriaga (1951: 41) and Lorey and Linares (1993: 1345); second series, Oliveira and Roberts (1998: 311)

Oliviera and Roberts (1998). While this concept is not perfectly congruent with the definition of middle class introduced in chapter 1, it is closer than the SALA series and produces estimates of similar magnitude (table 2.1).[5] Defined in these terms, the middle class comprised only 4.5 percent of the population in 1940 but had grown to over 13 percent by 1980. Measured by either standard, the middle class grew at a rapid pace during the Growth Era.

As the middle class grew, its character changed. The proportion of independent professionals, business owners, and medium farmers shrank relative to the rapidly growing numbers of dependent (salaried) managers, professionals, and semi-professionals. The shift from an independent to a dependent middle class, typical of modernizing economies, is spurred by the growth of government and the increasing scale of private enterprises. It is linked to a broader transition from property to occupation as the main basis of stratification. In Mexico, according to Iturriaga (1951), this process was well under way in the early decades of the twentieth century. However, the occupational statistics assembled by Oliveira and Roberts (1998: 311) suggest that the major shift came during the Growth Decades. The proportion of salaried professionals, managers, and semiprofessionals in their higher non-manual category rose from 27 percent in 1940 to 73 percent in 1980.

Social Mobility

"In today's Mexico," observed sociologist Pablo Gonzalez Casanova in 1962, "which is being industrialized and urbanized, there is permanent social mobility. The peasants of yesterday are today's workers, and the workers' children can be professionals" (quoted in Lorey

1993: 6). Some of the experiences related in the next section seem to fit Gonzalez Casanova's two-generation rural-to-urban, peasant-to-professional conception. Among middle-class respondents in Cuernavaca who entered the labor force during the Growth Decades or married someone who did, 40 percent grew up in popular-class homes and 60 percent in middle-class homes. This suggests that the Mexican middle class is diverse in its origins—as it more or less inevitably would be, given its rapid expansion.

The available studies of intergenerational occupational mobility confirm that the Growth Era was a time of rising mobility, though they also reveal that most Mexicans advanced modestly, if at all, over their parents' position. A recent survey asked men born in the periods 1936–38 and 1951–53 what their occupations were at age twenty-nine and what their father's occupation had been when the respondents were fifteen. The early careers of the men in these two birth cohorts would have played out during the Growth Era. Especially for the younger cohort, the survey revealed a high rate of father-to-son mobility (table 2.2). For both, upward mobility was greater than downward mobility.[6] But many men remained where they started. And more detailed statistics, not shown in the table, indicate that most upward mobility did not cross the manual/non-manual line, but involved movement among manual categories or among white-collar categories—for example, the peasant's son who becomes a factory worker or the retail sales clerk's son who becomes a lawyer (Zenteno 2002). Mobility into the still small middle class cannot have accounted for much of total mobility. If we assume, for example, that about 20 percent of the population is middle class and half of the middle class is recruited from lower classes, this means that only 10 percent of the population has been upwardly mobile into the middle class.

Paths to the Middle Class

Nearly half of my Cuernavaca respondents attended private schools, which suggests that they were raised in well-established middle-class (if not upper-class) families. Most of the others grew up in less privileged circumstances and seized the opportunities offered by the Growth Decades to gain, regain, or strengthen middle-class status.

TABLE 2.2   Occupational mobility (in percent)

Mobility	Birth cohort	
	1936–1938	1951–1953
Upward	35	50
Stable	48	38
Downward	17	11
Total	100	100

Source: Zenteno 2002
Note: Percentages have been rounded and may not total exactly 100.

Their lives, as related in interviews, reflect the twists and turns of Mexican history and the accidents of personal fortune.

Francisco Alarcón, for example, attended a public high school in San Antonio, Texas. His father, a Porfirian diplomat, had perished in the revolution, leaving his wife and children destitute. They fled to San Antonio, where his mother took in laundry to support the family. Alarcón later returned to Mexico City, took a job with a wealthy uncle, and worked his way through law school. His legal career would be propelled by the one significant asset he brought back from Texas: fluency in English. With American and Mexican partners, he founded a law firm in the mid-1940s to serve the American companies whose investments the Mexican government was avidly courting. Their lucrative practice permitted Alarcón to live well and sent his sons to private schools where English was the language of instruction. They would later start their own law firm, with a similar clientele.

Florencio Muñoz, the future Coca-Cola salesman, had a similarly inauspicious childhood. His father, a government employee in a provincial city, died when he was two. Florencio's mother moved the family to Mexico City, where she worked in a factory owned by a family friend and Florencio attended city schools. After completing *secundaria* (the equivalent of middle school), he took a first job as a sales clerk. Muñoz soon found his true vocation as a traveling salesman, and was employed for three decades by a succession of local and foreign firms. These positions reflected the needs of a dynamic national economy, radiating outward from Mexico City. Muñoz took pride in his career, but years later, his son Julio, from the perspective of a successful young professional, recalled that he and his seven siblings slept two to a bed in a house of flimsy construction. He describes their existence as "modest" and "lower middle class."

While Florencio Muñoz was traveling for Coca-Cola, *Ricardo Tijerino* was employed as a clerk in a Cuernavaca fabric shop. In 1947, he opened his own store in the center of town. A year later he married Carmen Blancas. Tijerino was the grandson of peasants and the son of a peddler with more children than he could afford. His wife was the illegitimate child of a domestic servant. Neither had finished primary school. But their business flourished as Cuernavaca's population soared and the local economy flourished in the 1960s and 1970s. By the late 1960s, they were able to build a large house with a swimming pool in an attractive upper-middle-class neighborhood and send their children to private schools. "I didn't want them to be illiterate like me," he would later claim. The Tijerinos paid for their children to travel and study abroad, though the couple never got farther than Acapulco until they retired.

Roberto Marín, a young teacher, came to Cuernavaca in 1960. Having grown up in Mexico City, he found the town quaint, perhaps a little backward. Marín's paternal grandparents were peasants who fled the violence of the revolution in the countryside for Mexico City, where they found work as domestics. His father worked variously as a messenger, bank guard, and school custodian. Roberto and his four siblings studied at least through secundaria. Two older sisters completed secretarial courses and found jobs with large firms. As their earnings lifted the family's fortunes, the Maríns dressed better and worried less about how to pay for the next meal. Roberto graduated from an academic *preparatoria* (equivalent of senior high school) with the hope of becoming an architect, but there was not enough money to sustain the years of training required. Instead, Roberto, his brother, and a younger sister entered a normal school and became teachers, a common path to the middle class.

Julio Bernal, the future doctor, and his family came to Cuernavaca, from the countryside, about the same time as Marín, but they had a very different perspective on the city. Life in Cuernavaca seemed luxurious to the Bernals, who marveled at the city's schools, electricity, and running water. Julio's father, who had worked in the fields until he was twenty, had just two years of education. The low-level civilian job he found with the police paid very little. But, like the Maríns and many other families, the Bernals enjoyed a rising standard of living as children came of age, joined the labor force, and contributed to the household's income. One sister worked as a domestic and later as a secretary, another as a seamstress. Their earnings also opened opportunities for the younger children.

As a younger male, Julio was allowed to focus on his education. He was ambitious and wanted to be "something, somebody"—perhaps a priest or a lawyer or a doctor. He liked the idea of defining right and wrong in law, but found out that lawyers were "corrupt." And he concluded that what the priests said contradicted what he was learning about science in school. From the age of thirteen he was fascinated by biology and this led him to medicine. Julio completed his education through medical school at public institutions.

Women's Paths

In Mexico's patriarchal society, women followed different paths to the middle class. In their narratives, men—fathers, lovers, husbands—loom large.

Manuela Prado's father bought and sold pigs and cattle in a small northern town to support a family of ten. When she was eight, her parents gave her to a great-aunt who had lost her only child—a gesture that remains both inexplicable and painful for Manuela decades later. Though she lived nearby, she would always feel like a stranger in her parents' home. She and her aunt survived, Manuela says, "on miracles." They raised a few pigs. Her aunt was friendly with local Indians, allowing them to park their animals on her property on market days, and they would sometimes give her "gifts" of beans or rice or invite her to share some tacos. Manuela studied through primary school, but there was no secondary school in the town. When she was thirteen, her aunt became very ill. Manuela nursed her for three years. After her death in the early 1960s, Manuela left for Mexico City, where she lived with a cousin and found work in a factory that produced electrical devices. She was, by her own account, still very much a child, who angered her cousin by spending her first week's pay on sweets. Manuela liked working in the factory. The employees, all women, were treated well. She appreciated the big mid-day meal

the company provided. While working there, she resumed her studies·
and completed secundaria.

Manuela met a young American who had come to Mexico to
study Spanish. The two shared a passion for music, and he helped her
pay the tuition for part-time study in a conservatory. They decided to
get married, and the American made four fruitless trips to the town
where she was born to ask her father for Manuela's hand. He refused,
saying that he did not want to lose his daughter. Conscious of the
irony of this belated paternal attachment, she was nonetheless unwill-
ing to disobey her father. She gave up the man who, it appears from
her telling, was the love of her life. By then, Manuela was working for
a group of opticians and in 1966 married one of the partners. After
taking a short course that taught her how to prescribe and make
eyeglasses, she began to operate two stores on her own. Their combined income would be sufficient to allow them to send their daughter to private schools and travel regularly to the United States and
Europe.

Susana Robles, born in 1949, grew up in Mexico City in circumstances no less painful than Manuela's, but her path to the middle
class was less circuitous. Susana's father was a union leader and later
operated a struggling retail business. He and his wife despised one
another. She was always ready to remind him that she was "white"
and he was dark-skinned. He accused her of infidelity and regularly
beat both his wife and their daughter. At age sixteen, Susana was
working for a small import firm. Her employer, a Frenchman who
had come to Mexico without resources in 1917 and built a lucrative
business, was quite taken with Susana. He was already in his seventies
when he appeared one day at her parents' door with a box of choco-
lates and proposal of marriage.

On her mother's advice, Susana seized the opportunity to escape
her father's house. They were married twenty days later. Still a bed
wetter in her teens, Susana feared that she would embarrass herself on
her wedding night.[7] But she did not and, liberated from her oppressive childhood, had no further problems. Susana and her husband
got along quite well. Before he died at age ninety-two, they had three
children, who were educated in private schools in Cuernavaca.

Amalia Vélez grew up in a northern city about the same time as
Manuela and Susana, but in a more placid and prosperous house-

hold. Her father, a man she describes as optimistic, hard working, and very traditional, was a mechanic, employed by PEMEX, the national oil monopoly, who rose to a supervisory job. His income was sufficient for the family to buy a car and send Amalia to a Catholic girls school, where she completed secundaria. She also trained to be bilingual secretary and, with her father's help, got a secretarial job at PEMEX. But her father would not allow her to continue her education, because there were no single-sex institutions in the city at preparatoria level, nor did he permit her to accept a year scholarship she was offered for study at a Catholic girls' school in Kentucky. The limits imposed on Amalia left her depressed. "They cut my wings," she says.

On a family vacation to Acapulco, Amalia met Aurelio Tijerino, son of the Cuernavaca merchants. When Amalia and Aurelio were married in 1976, the Tijerinos gave the young couple a car and money to start their own retail store. Amalia became an active partner in the business. Though never as successful as her in-laws' business, the store would provide the couple and their children a comfortable living for many years.

Angela Picón's path to the middle class comes closest to the male pattern of mobility. Angela's grandparents were peasants, fishermen, and domestics. Around 1950, her father's family moved to Mexico City, where Angela grew up. Her parents, who operated a small cafe, urged their four daughters and two sons to get university educations. All six began, but only the daughters managed to complete their degrees. Angela received a medical degree in 1979 and married another physician. They have lived well, but not extravagantly, on a combination of government employment and private practice. Their daughter, with no particular encouragement from her parents, has begun medical school.

Most of the people profiled in this and the preceding section, like others I interviewed in Cuernavaca, are one or two generations removed from the countryside. They grew up in urban popular-class households, typically in Mexico City. Far from affluent, they began full-time work at an early age or strained to stay in school with the help of older siblings, as did Bernal and Marín. Like millions of other Mexicans, they took advantage of the growing cities, the expanding public education system, and the booming economy of the Growth

Decades to lift themselves into the middle class. In this environment, young Julio Bernal and Angela Picón could imagine themselves becoming doctors, schooled at public expense. Two generations of Tijerinos and the Frenchman who married Susana Robles could build thriving retail businesses. And, in their different ways, lawyer Alarcón and traveling Coca-Cola salesman Florencio Muñoz could prosper serving foreign companies.

Women in this period shared in the general prosperity, but their lives were constrained. They were not invited to believe that they could "be someone" (or if they did, they risked having their "wings clipped"). Susana Robles, Manuela Prado, and Amalia Vélez all advanced themselves through marriage. And, although Susana and Amalia contributed importantly to the family businesses, they did so in a subordinate position. Even Angela Picón's medical career tended to be subordinated to her husband's.

But all four women have daughters who, like most of the young women in the families studied, are pursuing university degrees and professional or business careers. The expectations of middle-class daughters and their parents have changed radically. This generation of middle-class women may be better educated than their brothers. Nationally, among young adults eighteen to twenty-two years old living in middle-class households, 55 percent of females, but less than 40 percent of males have completed at least a year of university studies (ENIGH-2000).

CHAPTER 3

From Growth to Neoliberalism

The Growth Era ended on August 12, 1982. That day, the government of José López Portillo startled finance ministers and bankers around the world with the announcement that Mexico would not be able to make payments on its considerable foreign debt. The announcement proved to be a pivotal event. It not only marked the end of the postwar miracle and beginning of a sustained period of economic stagnation, but also set the stage for a fundamental restructuring of the national economy with profound implications for Mexicans of all classes.

Neoliberalism in Mexico

The 1982 debt crisis came on the heels of an economic boom propelled by high international oil prices and heavy borrowing abroad during the López Portillo years. When world oil prices fell and interest rates rose, the collapse was inevitable. But many observers, especially within Mexico's governing elite and political and financial institutions abroad, read the crisis as a sign of the exhaustion of the inwardly oriented developmentalist economic model that had guided the economy since the 1940s.

In the wake of the debt crisis, Mexico moved increasingly toward a neoliberal economic model. To obtain new financing, Mexico adopted an austerity program supported by the International Monetary Fund (IMF) that included sharp devaluation of the peso and deep cuts in government spending. Predictably, the immediate results were high inflation, falling real wages, rising unemployment, and two years of declining GDP. In the late 1980s and early 1990s, Mexico embraced more fundamental free-market reforms. These included privatization of state-owned enterprises (among them, the nation's banks, nationalized by López Portillo in 1982), abandonment of the decades-old agrarian reform program, liberalization of financial markets, deregulation of certain economic sectors, and reduction of barriers to foreign investment. Above all, Mexico opened itself to the world economy. It lowered or eliminated the tariffs and other barriers to trade that had been essential to the domestically oriented developmentalist model. Mexico entered the General Agreement on Tariffs and Trade (GATT) in 1986 and joined with the United States and Canada in the North American Free Trade Agreement (NAFTA) in January 1994.

The 1980s came to be known in Mexico, as elsewhere in Latin America, as "the lost decade." From 1981 to 1990, the Mexican economy grew at an almost invisible average rate of 0.8 percent (Ffrench-Davis et al. 1998: 178). How did the middle class fare during the lost decade? At first, probably worse than the rest of the population. The available income statistics indicate that in 1984 the real median household income for each of the lowest seven deciles was higher or about the same as it had been in 1977. For the top three deciles, the bracket that encompasses the middle class, incomes were lower in 1984 than in 1977. It is likely that many middle-class households experienced an abrupt reversal of fortunes in 1982. During the boom years 1977 to 1982, the total number of passenger cars registered in Mexico surged 68 percent and then stagnated for five years. Considered together, the income and car data suggest a period of rapidly rising middle-class incomes followed by a dramatic decline set off by the debt crisis (Rubalcava 1999: 153; World Motor Vehicle Data 1998: 213).

But the fortunes of middle-class families improved markedly in the late 1980s and early 1990s. ENIGH data reveals that the real median income of middle-class households rose 65 percent between 1984 and 1994.[1] In recent interviews, middle-class Cuernavacans recall that their businesses, professional practices, and salaries recovered quickly from the effects of the 1982 debt crisis. Most remember the period that followed as a time of growing prosperity.

Middle-Class Fortunes

Dr. Ricardo Lambert describes the years 1982 to 1994 as "*mi época de oro*—my golden age." These were the best years in several decades of a successful specialist medical practice. In the 1960s, he recalls, there were plenty of patients. In the 1970s, there were fewer patients but they were more affluent. In the 1980s and early 1990s, there were large numbers of patients and they had money to pay for medical care. These patients were, by and large, middle class; the wealthy could fly to Houston when they needed a specialist. By 1980, Lambert had built his dream house in an elegant neighborhood of Cuernavaca, traveled with his wife to Europe, and taken the whole family to Disneyland in California. His standard of living did not change after the 1982 debt crisis. He was able to continue traveling, send his three children to expensive private schools and universities, and accumulate substantial savings for his retirement.

Julio Bernal, the Cuernavaca schoolboy who wanted to "be somebody" was able to live much better than his peasant grandparents or his working-class parents had, though he often felt financially pressed. Bernal completed his medical training in the late 1970s, returned to Cuernavaca, and found a job in the public health care system. He lived with his parents until he was married in 1982. Bernal's wife, a nurse also employed in the public sector, continued working. The debt crisis seems to have had little effect on them. The new couple bought a small but attractive home in a pleasant middle-class neighborhood, with loans they obtained as state employees. They were able to send their daughters, born in 1983 and 1985, to good private schools. Wanting to reserve time for his family, Bernal did not start a private practice in addition to his public sector practice as Lambert and many other Mexican physicians did. His salary rose as he assumed administrative responsibilities, but so did the family's expenses. In particular, tuition costs climbed as his daughters advanced from kindergarten to primary to secondary school. It seemed to Bernal that they were broke at the end of every pay period. Only the traditional extra month's salary (the *aguinaldo*), paid in December, allowed them to catch up on bills and pay for the family vacation in Acapulco.

Fernando Blandón started his contracting business in the less than propitious year of 1982. But by 1985, the firm was thriving, as it would be, more or less continuously, until 1994. Despite increasing competition and a substantial loss of savings in the 1987 collapse of the Mexican stock market, he was able to build a 5,000-square-foot house for his family, without a mortgage, by stretching the construction over four years. During the same period, he and his wife kept their two children in private schools and bought a succession of increasingly expensive automobiles. Blandón also felt prosperous enough to establish a second household with another woman—in Mexican parlance, a *casa chica*.

The Garcias, both public school teachers, were married in 1992. Their combined salaries seemed ample at the time. Within two years, they had their first child, bought a new subcompact car, and completed much of the construction of a home on land her father had given them as a wedding present.

Travel abroad, increasingly common in this period, was a sure mark of middle-class success. The trip to *Disneylandia* was close to mandatory for prosperous middle-class families with children. The Blandóns followed the Lamberts there. Amalia and Aurelio Tijerino, the Cuernavaca merchants, visited Disneyland twice with their children. The Tijerinos also took up skiing in the 1980s, traveling repeatedly to the famous Taos ski area in New Mexico. From 1988 to 1994, Ramon Lavalle, a divorced non-custodial father, took long annual trips with his three children. They saw Disneyland but also the Metropolitan Museum in New York, the Louvre in Paris, the Uffizi in Florence, Gaudi's *Sagrada Familia* in Barcelona, and William Shakespeare's home in Stratford. These same families also vacationed in Mexico, as did many less affluent middle-class families. The beach resort at Acapulco was the favored national destination for the middle-class Cuernavacan. During this period, a vacation there was within the reach of most of the city's middle-class families.

The Peso Crisis and the Income Shock

This fondly remembered era of middle-class prosperity came to an unexpected end in December 1994, as the Mexican government struggled to stabilize the tumbling value of the peso. What came to be known as the Peso Crisis[2] precipitated a broader economic crisis.

The neoliberal policies that Mexico adopted in the 1980s and early 1990s had yielded mixed results. GDP growth, erratic at first, improved after 1988. The budget deficit nearly disappeared, and inflation declined to comfortable levels. At the same time, poverty rates increased, along with income inequality. Mexico's opening to the global economy stimulated a steep rise in exports. But export income was more than offset by rapid growth in imports. Mexico was flooded with foreign investment. But much of it took the form of speculative portfolio investment, which could quickly evaporate. In late 1994, the peso was increasingly overvalued. Whether because of economic mismanagement by the outgoing Salinas administration or more fundamental flaws in the neoliberal economic model, the economy was obviously vulnerable.

In the wake of the Peso Crisis, Mexico was compelled, as it had been in 1982, to seek emergency help abroad and adopt painful stabilization measures, beginning with a drastic devaluation of the peso. In 1995 the Mexican economy suffered its worst contraction since the 1930s. Middle-class households suffered a loss of income so abrupt, so deep and so traumatizing that it can be described as an income shock: between 1994 and 1996, the median middle-class income plunged 40 percent.[3]

Effects of the Crisis on Cuernavaca Families

Most of the fifty-two middle-class families interviewed in Cuernavaca report significant economic losses in the period following the 1994 devaluation. The damage was widespread, affecting majorities of middle-class households headed by the young and the old, the more and the less educated, businesspeople and professionals, privately and publicly employed, the upwardly mobile and the well born. Only one in five families experienced little or no loss. For the majority, the damage was sufficient to require substantial changes in consumption habits. A few were reduced to living on a fraction of their accustomed incomes.

The experience left middle-class Cuernavacans in a cynical mood, as I discovered when I started interviewing them five years after the devaluation. Respondents were told in advance that I was writing a book about the middle class and was especially interested in the effects of the economic crisis on middle-class families. Many began the interview with a facetious comment, along the lines of, "What middle class? That class is finished," as if we were talking about some vanishing stone-age tribe. In retrospect, such remarks were indicative of the growing disaffection that would turn middle-class Mexicans against the PRI.

Whatever their opinions about the state of the middle class, they were able to describe, in detail, the economic effects of the crisis on their own families. They spoke of struggling small businesses, shrunken professional practices, and salaries eroded by rapid inflation. A few had lost their jobs. Some families lost mortgaged homes or real estate investments to surging interest rates. Some owners of small commercial properties, including several retirees, lost rental income to vacancies, late payments, and inflation.

Here are a few illustrative cases, including households that suffered severe damage and others whose losses were minimal or transitory.

Aurelio and Amalia Tijerino, the merchants whose thriving business supported family vacations to Disneyland and Taos in the early 1990s, could barely keep their business and household afloat after the Peso Crisis. Economic stagnation and growing competition cut into profits. One day, a 5,000-peso check to a major supplier bounced. The Tijerinos daily preoccupation was finding enough money to keep their children in expensive private schools.

Eduardo Rojas owned several retail shops, with more than twenty employees in the 1980s. He earned enough to take long trips to Europe with his wife. But even before the crisis, heavy competition from national chains in his sector was eroding his profits. In the mid-1990s, Rojas was reduced to operating a struggling "minimart" out of his home, which could be seized at any moment by the bank holding his mortgage. He employed no one and could not afford to drive his aging automobile.

Francisco Alarcón, who mastered English in a Texas high school and started a lucrative law practice in the late 1940s, was still in practice with his sons in the mid-1990s. Because their most important clients were foreign corporations that could still afford to pay for legal advice, the economic crisis had little effect on their income.

Efraín Martínez, an attorney with a largely local practice in criminal and administrative law, had fewer, less prosperous clients, after 1994. His practice produced about half the income it had prior to the crisis.

Julio Muñoz is a young veterinarian. Most of his clients are middle-class pet owners. Julio is a careful financial manager. When he left the employ of an established vet to start his own practice, he decided to focus on house calls and defer the high costs associated with operating a clinic. His growing practice stagnated in the wake of the devaluation, but soon recovered.

The Mirandas are both doctors. Before the crisis they started a private practice, while also working for the state. But their practice collapsed with the crisis, leaving them wholly dependent on government employment; and they lost a new home, on which they had made a 66 percent down payment, when interest rates spiked.[4]

Dr. Lambert still maintained a busy private practice in the early 1990s. After the Peso Crisis he continued going to his office daily, more or less out of habit, to see two to four patients. A building he and his wife owned was partially empty and two units were occupied by family members, who do not pay rent.

Pedro Joaquin Villanueva, a bank manager, says his company prospered in the wake of the crisis. Pedro Joaquin survived a 30 percent downsizing of its labor force, which, he says, strengthened the bank. But his salary lagged inflation. And he was a victim of the sudden rise in interest rates, losing most of his investment in the apartment he had purchased when he managed a branch in Acapulco.

The Garcias, the two young teachers married in 1992, watched the value of their salaries shrink in the late 1990s. Fortunately, the loans they had taken out to buy a subcompact car and build a home were not subject to big interest rate hikes. Construction on the house was suspended, but the family was able to move into the completed first floor.

As these cases suggest, the consequences of the crisis for families depend on both domestic and market characteristics. The key domestic characteristics were domestic cycle status and home ownership.[5] Young families with school-age children (the Tijerinos) and families with variable rate mortgages (the Mirandas) were especially vulnerable. Older families and those who owned their homes outright or had access to (relatively rare) fixed rate financing (the Garcias, Lambert) were safer.

The varied fortunes of independent professionals and merchants illustrate the importance of market characteristics. Lawyer Martinez and the doctors saw their practices shrink along with the incomes of their financially stressed, middle-class clients. But Alarcón, dependent on foreign clients, was relatively immune to the crisis. Among merchants, the effects of the economic contraction were most devastating for retailers like Eduardo Rojas, competing in sectors already challenged by low-cost national chain stores.

Young adults in these families have especially felt the effects of the crisis—though more as stagnation than loss. Many university educated men and women in their twenties and thirties remained financially dependent on parents and in-laws in the late 1990s. Some expressed frustration that careers they began with high expectations were stalled or, it seems, abruptly ended.

Laura de la Puente, in her early thirties and recently married, grew up in a prosperous upper-middle-class home. An academic star, she earned engineering and MBA degrees at a prestigious private institution. After working in a couple of corporate jobs, she started a business of her own, which has struggled since 1995. She has tried and failed to find another corporate job. Both she and a brother, who also feels thwarted in his career, cannot afford homes of their own—a milestone, they are painfully aware, their parents had passed by this point in their lives. They and, according to Laura, many of their friends, were learning that they could not depend on the rising arc of earnings that they had regarded as a middle-class birthright. "People who have not had a good life, people who have not traveled, expect less," she says, through tears. "[My] expectations are high and [my] possibilities are limited."

Ramiro Moreno, about the same age as Laura, did not begin life with her advantages, but also had high hopes for a career. He earned an electrical engineering degree (*licenciatura*) from a state university with determined help from his peasant family. But the only job he was able to find was teaching in a preparatory-level technical school. He and his wife, who was teaching half-time, could barely earn a middle-class income. Ramiro, his parents, and his friends all believed that study would give them a big economic advantage. "But now I'm not so sure. My generation doesn't think the way we did before."

CHAPTER 4

Magicians

Surviving the Crisis of the 1990s

We Mexicans are magicians," a small-business owner told me in 1999. What he had in mind was not Castaneda's mysterious Don Juan but the unnatural ability of his compatriots to survive the economic upheavals of recent years. This chapter examines the economic survival strategies of middle-class families in the mid- to late 1990s. The topic opens a window on middle-class life. People reveal themselves under stress. Threatened, they employ whatever resources they possess to defend themselves. Forced to make choices, to yield some things in order to save others, they expose their ultimate priorities.

The Middle-Class Response

The response of middle-class Cuernavaca households to the economic crisis falls under two broad rubrics: a budget strategy and a capital strategy. The first refers to attempts to adjust spending to new realities and find new sources of income, and the second to efforts to mobilize the various forms of capital available to middle-class families.

Capital is value accumulated over time and capable of yielding future benefits to its owner. Middle-class capital strategy can usefully be understood in terms of the three forms of capital distinguished by sociologist Pierre Bourdieu (1986): *economic capital,* the basic, monetary form of capital, institutionalized as property rights; *cultural capital,* knowledge in its broadest sense, institutionalized in educational credentials;[1] and *social capital,* mutual obligations embodied in social networks such as kinship, friendship, and group membership. The value of the various forms of capital is enhanced by the potential of each for transformation into the others—a process that Bourdieu, invoking liturgical language, calls "transubstantiation." When, for example, a middle-class family draws financial help from relatives, social capital is transformed into economic capital.

Bourdieu's concepts may seem vague or overly broad. Cultural capital covers a vast territory ranging from table manners to advanced degrees. The relationship of economic capital to established concepts such as earnings, income, and net worth is often unclear. But by extending the concept of capital beyond the narrowly economic, Bourdieu strengthens our understanding of class reproduction. From Bourdieu's perspective, the sum of the various capitals is the cumulative advantage of the privileged classes—developed over time, sometimes generations, and shared by the members of a family, a social network or an entire class.

As the next few pages will show, Cuernavaca's middle-class families leaned heavily on accumulated social and economic capital to survive the economic crisis of the late 1990s. They also cut consumption in many areas, but continued to spend large sums on developing cultural capital in the form of education for their children.

Adjusting Consumption

Most of the families interviewed say that they reduced consumption as a result of the economic crisis. Javier Pardo, an older physician, described in some detail the adjustments he and his family were forced to make. The Pardos were accustomed to living well. They bought new cars regularly and took two vacations a year—one to the United States and one within Mexico. Such luxuries were no longer possible. But it was the petty concessions to the crisis that most grated on Dr. Pardo.

> Until three years ago, I did not resole my shoes. Now I resole each pair of shoes three times. I know shoes, but I no longer buy the Florsheim shoes I like, but cheaper ones. We [used to] go to Vips or Sanborns a couple of times a week—now, maybe two times a year. We've cut expenses by not going to the movies, by not having coffee with friends, by buying cheaper clothes. I'll buy a

60-peso pair of cheap cotton pants at the Comercial Mexicana, instead of the 200-peso pants I used to buy. I have one pair of the better ones I hold in reserve for special occasions. The car is ten years old. I go to the supermarket and just buy basic things, cheap. No luxuries. Whatever cheese is on sale. Not the cheapest toilet paper, which is like sandpaper, but something only slightly above that. Not the 90-peso/kilo ham, but the 25-peso stuff, and who knows what's in it.

Middle-class Mexicans were startled to learn that there were small things, like decent toilet paper, that they could no longer afford. A professional woman says that she no longer buys "Buen Hogar" (*Good Housekeeping*). She also recalled wanting to buy a snow cone one day and deciding no, she really couldn't afford it, and then thinking how strange that was. A teacher reported that she sometimes runs out of laundry detergent and money, and must go several days without doing the wash. A consultant used to buy large quantities of ham and make "fat sandwiches"; after December 1994, the sandwiches were thin. Many respondents say that they used to go to the supermarket and buy whatever appealed to them. They learned to limit themselves to "only the indispensable." The discovery that they must avoid what they call "superficial expenses" was unsettling for many middle-class adults. It threatened their sense of who they were.

The variety of forgone consumption was considerable. The crisis forced contractor Blandón to give up his mistress. The casa chica was absorbing a quarter of his shrinking income—an expenditure difficult to justify, if only because he and his wife were weighing pulling their daughter out of an expensive private university. Families reported eating less meat, spending less on clothing, reducing or eliminating their dependence on domestic servants, and struggling to control phone bills. They deferred the purchase of new automobiles and, in at least some cases, canceled auto insurance. Two families lost uninsured cars to thieves and could not afford to replace them. Like the Pardos, many families sharply cut expenditures for diversions such as restaurant meals, day trips, movies, and late-afternoon coffees.

Forgone vacations were probably the most sensitive indicators of the economic misfortunes of the middle class. The family trip to Acapulco, Ixtapa, San Antonio, New York, or Paris is regarded as an

important measure of relative prosperity. Respondents fondly recalled pre-crisis vacations. But these middle-class Mexicans were
traveling less frequently, to cheaper, nearer destinations (not New
York or even San Antonio, but Acapulco or Vera Cruz). Many families gave up vacation travel altogether.

But Not Education: Building Cultural Capital

The expenditures that households maintained under economic adversity, like the ones they chose to sacrifice, reveal much about the
character of middle-class life. In her study of middle-class responses
to the crisis of the early 1980s, Gonzales de la Rocha (1995) noted that
families were especially reluctant to give up private substitutes for
public services, including medical care, transportation, and education. In the late 1990s, most middle class Cuernavacans continued to
use private physicians and move about town in their own, sometimes
aging, vehicles. But their observations suggest that these preferences
were largely matters of convenience. Their attachment to private education is more passionate.

Virtually all the school-age children in the households studied
were enrolled in private institutions. Not one family reported shifting
a child to a public school as a result of the crisis. This pattern was
apparently typical. According to data provided by the state education
department, private school enrollments in Cuernavaca barely registered the economic shock of 1995 and were slightly higher as a percentage of total school enrollment in 1998 than they had been in 1994
(table 4.1).

Private school tuitions in Mexico are high relative to typical
middle-class incomes, and there is little in the way of tuition support.
A family with two or three kids in school and a middling middle-class
income around 15,000 pesos could easily spend a quarter to a third of
its income on schooling—a proportion that would, of course, tend to
rise as income declined in a crisis. A few families indicated that they
had shifted to schools with lower tuitions. One single mother whose
income plunged in the crisis was forced to move her primary-school
age daughter through four successively cheaper private schools. The
daughter, according to her mother, accepted the transfers with good
grace, insisting only that she not be placed in a public school.

TABLE 4.1   Private school enrollment in Cuernavaca

	1994	1995	1996	1997	1998
Primary grades (6 years)					
Private school students	8,859	8,500	8,595	8,761	9,127
As percent of all students	19.2	18.5	18.7	19.3	20.3
Secondary grades (3 years)					
Private school students	3,612	3,541	3,516	3,718	3,965
As percent of all students	18.6	18.0	18.1	19.2	20.4

Source: Calculated from data provided by Morelos State, Instituto de Educación Básica

Asked to explain why they insist on private schooling for their children, financially pressed parents emphasize that a good education is an "investment," essential for a successful middle-class career. "Education is the only thing we can give our children," runs a common refrain—reflecting an awareness that families in the new Mexico can no longer transmit middle-class status to their children via inherited land or family enterprises. Their views recall Bourdieu's conception of education as cultural capital.

According to these respondents, private schools offer a superior curriculum (in particular, students learn to speak English), a more disciplined atmosphere, and more desirable schoolmates. In public schools, they say, teachers may or may not show up, pay little attention to their students' progress, and fail to control their behavior.

Their descriptions of public school students express a great social distance from "the children of workers and taxi drivers"; "people with other customs—for example, the parents beat their children"; families with "little culture." In contrast, private school students are "the children of doctors—people with [higher] aspirations." These are people whom it is useful to know. "Here in Mexico," observes a mother straining to keep her kids in private schools, "friendships count."

A growing preference for private higher education was also evident in the interviews. Many middle-class Cuernavacans believe that employers prefer to hire graduates of private universities. A bank manager, the son of peasants, whose own young son attends an expensive private school, confirms this. The bank, he says, is not likely to hire from the University of Morelos, when graduates of the local branch of the private Monterrey Institute of Technology are available, and, he believes, most large firms operating in the Cuernavaca area take a similar approach. But private university tuitions are well beyond the reach of many middle-class families. Nonetheless, nearly half of the college students in the families interviewed attend private universities.

Finding New Sources of Income

Some of the Cuernavaca families attempted to recover earnings lost to the crisis by tapping new sources of income. Here are some examples:

Hosting. Three of the families contracted with a local Spanish language school to house and host foreign students. This activity turns an attractive middle-class home into a commercial asset. But the program is time consuming, especially for the wife, who bears most of the added burden of cooking and chauffeuring, and the financial compensation is modest (perhaps 2,000 pesos per student per month after the costs of food).

Retailing. Marta Ruíz and Rosa Portales (married women with working husbands) started their own retail stores, catering to middle-class patrons. Portales had been working part-time and caring for two small children. Ruíz had been working mornings as a teacher in a private school and continued to do so, having persuaded her mother to mind the store during the hours she taught. After a year both enterprises seemed fairly successful. Portales was considering giving up her teaching job.

Aurelio Tijerino, the financially pressed Cuernavaca merchant mentioned earlier, was less successful with a second, small shop he opened in a nearby village. The considerable effort it required was hardly worth the meager income it produced.

Scaling down. Carla Banquero rented her large home and moved into a much smaller house, which she also owned. The move brought in new income and enabled the family to save part of what they were spending on domestics.

Back to the land. Lawyer Efraín Martínez fell back on his peasant origins to supplement the income from a practice sharply reduced by the crisis. With the help of paid laborers, he intensified the cultivation of land inherited from his parents, producing staple crops for his family and a high-value commercial crop for the Cuernavaca market (pipian seeds, used to produce *mole*). "Some day," he gravely predicts, "we'll have to depend on our own production to survive."

Few of the middle-class families I interviewed responded to economic stress by increasing their participation in the labor force. About half the adult women—most notably, younger women—work outside the home. But almost all began their careers prior to the crisis. They do not want their teenage children to work, preferring that they focus on their studies. Fifteen- to seventeen-year-olds in middle-class Mexican families are, in fact, less likely to work than their American peers in the top half of the income distribution (ENIGH-2000; U.S. Department of Labor 2000).

None of the families seriously considered seeking employment in the United States. Research on this alternative faces an obvious sampling problem: entire households that have migrated are not available for study. However, the interviews included questions about the careers of respondents' siblings and adult children, a numerous population, among whom only four individuals had ever worked in the United States. Three of the four were young adults with modest levels of education who found low-skill jobs in the States. Most middle-class Mexicans have accumulated significant economic, social, and cultural capital at home. They own real estate and business assets, have supportive social networks, and possess educational credentials—all valuable in Mexico, but difficult to liquidate or transfer abroad.

In sum, other than families with members who left one job or business for another, fewer than a dozen of the fifty-two households found new sources of income. Rather than bolstering income, families were spending less and drawing on accumulated capital.

Social Capital: The Kindness of Kin

Susana del Valle and her husband, a well-educated young couple with a four-year-old son, became heavily dependent on support from kin in the wake of the 1994 devaluation. Unemployed and unhoused, they received financial help from both families and lived with a succession of aunts until they finally found jobs. They continue to receive occasional emergency help from their families when confronted with bills they cannot cover. A brother with a high-paying corporate job in Houston has been especially generous.

Angela Rubio, the divorced custodial mother of children ages six and nine, could not meet her family's needs with her salary and modest child support payments. Angela and her children frequently ate with her mother, who lives nearby. They received medical care from cousins who are a GP and a pediatrician. For a year, another relative loaned them a house. In financial emergencies, she turned to her grandmother and a male friend.

Francisco Valdivia and his wife, Maria Elena, both had steady jobs—she as a secretary and he as a low-level public administrator— that paid a total of 10,500 pesos per month. But they and their three small children received a continuous flow of family help. His mother and brother paid for the children's clothing. The Valdivias borrowed from her to meet emergencies, such as an extra large credit card bill, which they paid back in installments. She was also helping them get a home loan. At the same time, Maria Elena and her siblings were helping a brother still in college, his girlfriend, and their (unplanned) child.

Like these three, many middle-class families depend on kin to help them survive periods of economic adversity. Support typically comes from parents and siblings and, less frequently, from aunts, uncles, and cousins. It takes varied forms, including cash, loans, help with tuition, professional services, meals, and housing. One family received a weekly allotment of five chickens from relatives in the poultry business. Five young entrepreneurs were operating businesses rent-free in commercial spaces owned by their parents; at least some of these enterprises could not otherwise survive. Two siblings and their young families occupied apartments in a family-owned building. As these examples suggest, the recipients of help were usually younger couples with children, who might be facing high private-school tuition costs.

Economic Capital: Living on
Accumulated Wealth

It appears that many of the households studied were maintaining a middle-class living standard in a period of economic crisis by drawing on their own or their families' accumulated wealth. A rigorous accounting of this tendency would require measurement of change in net worth. The relevant evidence gathered in this study is less precise, but certainly suggestive. For example, an older professional estimated that he was spending twice as much as he was earning. A merchant said that he was selling down his valuable inventory in order to meet household expenses. Another retailer indicated that he had sold three cars to liquidate debts to his suppliers. Some households had incurred significant credit card debt. The average age of the cars driven by these middle-class families increased with the crisis.

Many families owned homes, cars, and, in some cases, commercial real estate, free of debt. Though these assets were depreciating over time, ownership bolstered a family's current standard of living. The young entrepreneurs mentioned earlier, who have free use of family-owned properties, were drawing on capital accumulated by the preceding generation to sustain their otherwise precarious businesses.

In the long run, these are self-limiting strategies. They may help a family through a difficult period. But at some point the house needs major repairs, the car dies, the credit card limit is breached, the inventory is consumed, savings dissipate, and the assets accumulated by the older generation must generate retirement income. Only economic revival can halt these processes of decay.

How the Middle Class Survives

If, as the man quoted at the beginning of this chapter suggests, Mexicans survive economic crisis by magic, their magic consists of the adroit exploitation of the diverse economic and social resources available to families. After December 1994, middle-class families in Cuernavaca adopted a survival strategy that (1) emphasized reduced consumption, rather than new income, (2) drew on accumulated economic and social capital, and (3) reserved resources for long-term investment in cultural capital, specifically formal education. Do these elements describe a uniquely middle-class survival strategy? The short answer is yes.

Of course, popular-class households also reduce consumption, draw on economic and social capital, and send their children to school, to the extent they are able, in times of economic stress. These households may, for example, borrow from neighbors and kin or exchange labor, such as baby-sitting and construction work on informal housing. But there are important differences between the typical popular- and middle-class patterns.[2]

Survival strategies inevitably reflect the large class disparities in resources. In the best of times, families of the popular majority have limited discretionary income and, therefore, few painless ways to cut spending in hard times. They are much more likely to depend on increased labor force participation to bolster the household budget. Since earnings from the jobs they typically hold vary little with skill or seniority, the number of employed household members is the main determinant of income, and there is strong incentive to push additional members of the household into the labor force.

In contrast, the extraordinary range of items that may be squeezed out of middle-class budgets—the restaurant meals forgone, the shoes resoled, the car insurance canceled, the mistress abandoned—suggests a considerable cushion of discretionary income. The lives and budgets of middle-class families are also cushioned by endowments of capital in its varied forms that far exceed the means available at lower class levels. In Cuernavaca, middle-class families spend savings, sell off inventories, and drive their cars beyond past limits. Younger families, in particular, depend on social capital: they turn to relatives for emergency loans, meals, rent-free housing or commercial space, professional services (the lawyer uncle, the cousin pediatrician), and help with private school tuitions.

There are also significant class differences in the types of social capital that households draw on. Research on the survival strategies of popular-class households reveals the importance of assistance from family, fictive kin, friends, and neighbors (Lomnitz 1977, Gonzalez de la Rocha 1994). In contrast, middle-class families in Cuernavaca seldom turn to friends, neighbors, or other peers. In need, middle-class families turn, almost exclusively, to close kin for help.

Because they typically have telephones and automobiles and often have domestics to whom they can entrust their homes and children for at least short periods, middle-class Mexicans are better able to maintain relationships with relatives who do not live in the immediate vicinity. They thus have little need or desire to enter into exchange relationships with neighbors (Willis 2000; Icazuriaga Montes 1994: 454).

A critical set of class differences in survival strategies revolve around work and education at the intermediate stages of the domestic cycle.[3] This is the point at which popular households defend or expand income by putting teenage members of the household into the labor force, while middle-class households, like those studied in Cuernavaca, are mobilizing all the resources available to them to keep their children out of the labor force and in school. Nationally, 88 percent of middle class fifteen- to seventeen-year-olds are in school, compared to 48 percent of their popular-class peers, according to the ENIGH-2000 data.[4] In Cuernavaca, younger middle-class families structure household budgets around tuition costs. Building cultural capital through education is obviously not a solution to a short-term economic crisis, but short-term strategy must accommodate to it.

Middle-class survival strategies in Cuernavaca are fundamentally different not simply because middle-class families draw on vastly superior resources, in different ways, but also because they have different objectives. Middle-class households do not struggle to put food on the table but to pay private school tuitions. Their survival strategies do not concern biological survival but the survival of a middle-class standard of living and its transmission across generations.

Recovering

By the end of the decade, there was increasing evidence of economic recovery in middle-class Cuernavaca. Fernando Blandón's contracting business, down 60 percent in the months after the devaluation, had rebounded. Oscar Contreras's fledgling dental practice, after a shaky start, was established and slowly growing. In 1999, Vicente Gonzalez felt confident enough to buy an expensive new SUV. His retail business had fallen sharply in 1995, but it was reviving. As we have seen, Susana del Valle, her husband, and their small son had survived for months on erratic earnings and family charity, but both found jobs in 1998. Efraín Martínez was able to replace the earnings lost to his shrunken legal practice with new farm income. Julio Muñoz's young veterinary practice had stagnated for a while but was growing again. Middle-class Cuernavacans, he found, were still willing to spend on their pets. In 1999, Muñoz was able to move his family into a new house.

By 2000, Cuernavaca's middle-class families had regained much but not all of the economic territory they lost in 1995. Many families were still struggling to constrain spending. Vacations were fewer and closer to home. Young families were, if anything, more worried about paying the costs of private education.

But even those who had successfully navigated the crisis of the mid-1990s emerged from the experience angry at a regime they had long supported.

CHAPTER 5

The Middle Class and
the Post-Revolutionary Regime

During the Growth Decades, Mexico's ruling party measured its success by the expansion and prosperity of the middle class. The PRI claimed the middle class as its own creation and expected gratitude in return. But by the early 1970s, party leaders feared that the middle class was slipping away. In a May 1975 speech inaugurating a party conference on the middle class, PRI president Jesús Reyes Heroles described the middle class as a source of "instability," with tendencies toward "fascism." Many PRIistas, he suggested, regard the middle class as less than patriotic, given to "conspicuous and extravagant consumption," and indifferent to the fate of the popular majority. But the party must win the loyalty of the middle class. Failure to do so, insisted Reyes Heroles, would expose the country to "counter-revolutionary consequences" (Reyes Heroles 1988) Underlying these remarks was a sense of betrayal by the middle class shared by many PRIistas.

The convening of the May 1975 conference exposed the regime's growing preoccupation with "the middle-class question." On October 1, José López Portillo, recently anointed by the outgoing chief executive as Mexico's president-to-be, addressed another party audience on the same topic. López Portillo presented himself as "a typical member of the middle class." He described the middle class as the creation and "fundamental aspiration" of his party. But he warned that the middle class was also literate, critical, empowered by its access to the mass media, and, therefore, a potential threat. The middle class must be organized, persuaded, and "reincorporated" into the political system. Here López Portillo referred to the "crisis of conscience of 1968, [which] was the crisis of conscience of the middle class" (López Portillo 1988). The allusion, certainly not lost on his audience, was to a prime source of their worry about the middle class. On October 2, 1968, seven years earlier, almost to the day, a protest movement led by middle-class students ended in the bloody Tlatelolco massacre.

PRIista anxieties about middle-class support in 1975 were not misplaced but premature. Relations between Mexico's rulers and the middle class had been problematic in the 1920s and 1930s. They would become so again toward the end of the century. In 2000, middle-class voters would play a decisive role in the defeat of the PRI, by then the longest surviving ruling party on the planet. But for most of the half-century after 1940, middle-class Mexicans, like their compatriots, were at once loyal, cynical, and passive in their attitudes toward the regime. They were loyal to a system that staked powerful symbolic claims to legitimacy and delivered real material benefits through economic growth, cynical about its day-to-day operations, but passive in the face of authoritarian rule unhesitatingly imposed from above. Their passivity reflected not only fear of the power that hovered over them, but also fear of a power vacuum. Especially for the older generations who remembered the violent years of the Mexican revolution or had heard vivid tales of the period, the power of the PRI was protection against political chaos.

The Post-Revolutionary Regime

The political system that emerged in the 1920s from the turmoil of the revolution and endured until 2000 was known to its partisans as "the Revolution" (always capitalized in print), a rambling concept connecting the government, the official party, and the related mass organizations with the 1910 rebellion. I will refer to this system as the post-revolutionary regime or, simply, the regime.

The key features of the post-revolutionary regime were (1) presidential power, (2) corporatist control of society, and (3) legitimation by the myth of the Revolution. There were few constraints on the power of Mexican presidents, other than the firmly held constitutional principle limiting the chief executive to one six-year term. Elections were, until the late 1980s, meaningless except as legitimizing rituals. Members of congress, judges, governors, generals, and leaders of the party were, in effect, selected by the president and subservient to him. Presidents also selected their own successors. A corporatist system of mass organizations tied to the regime, such as the official labor unions, functioned to control (rather then represent) workers, peasants, and other popular social sectors. These organizations mobilized their members for elections and other political purposes, while limiting the demands they made on the system. The myth of a continuing Revolution, guided by the PRI, was relentlessly propagated through the mass organizations, the schools, the media, and public rituals. It permitted Mexico's generally conservative, authoritarian rulers to pose as the political heirs of democrat Francisco Madero, agrarian rebel Emiliano Zapata, and other heroes of the 1910 revolution; to identify themselves with the agrarian reform and the (wildly popular) nationalization of the petroleum industry in the 1930s; and to claim credit for the spectacular economic expansion of the postwar years. The myth of the Revolution promised future triumphs built on past glories.

A caveat: "post-revolutionary" as used here refers to the more or less stable system of power that prevailed in Mexico, not to the fluctuating ideological complexion of the party and successive governments.

In the Wake of the Revolution

Historians of the upheaval that transformed Mexico after 1910 describe two parallel revolutions: a political revolution with a largely middle-class following and a social revolution propelled by the anger of dispossessed peasants. Both were opposed to the old regime of Porfirio Díaz, but (simplifying slightly) it can be said that most of the armed violence and political fury of the years 1910 to 1940 was devoted to sorting out the competing claims and personalities of these two class-based movements.

From the late 1920s to the late 1930s, the political tides ran against the middle class. Official rhetoric denounced the middle class as a remnant of the old regime, and the official party, launched in 1929, defined itself as an organization serving workers and peasants. Middle-class Catholics were alarmed by the regime's severe (sometimes violent) anticlerical policies. These included the imposition of a secular curriculum on all schools, including the private Catholic institutions that taught many middle-class children. During this period, argues Soledad Loaeza (1988), the urban middle class became the implicit political ally of the Church.

In the 1930s, church-state conflict subsided, but social policy took a radical turn. Especially under Lázaro Cárdenas (1934–1940), government rhetoric and policy strongly favored the popular majority to the disadvantage of the middle class. Peasants and workers were encouraged to organize to defend their own interests. In the city, strikes were common. In the countryside, millions of acres were redistributed to peasant communities. During this period, middle-class opposition groups were thwarted, sometimes violently by the regime and its supporters. In 1940, the popular presidential candidacy of Juan Andreu Almazán drew significant middle-class support. The campaign was marred by street clashes between partisans of Almazán and Manuel Avila Camacho, the candidate of the ruling party. Avila Camacho won a lopsided victory, according to official returns that few observers believed. But one middle-class political organization that emerged during this period would survive and triumph decades later: the National Action Party (PAN).

The Politics of Growth

Even before Cárdenas left office, the political tide was turning. Especially after World War II, the regime's overriding objective was the promotion of capitalist economic development, in both the cities and the countryside. Unions affiliated with the official party were transformed into a mechanism to constrain labor militancy. The agrarian reform laws were modified to protect commercial agriculture and the pace of land expropriations slowed. Growth was to be favored over redistribution in the new era. In the mid-1930s, Cárdenas had committed his government to "the great cause of social reform." Now, Miguel Alemán (1946–1952), the president most identified with the new direction, said that what he wanted was for "all Mexicans to have a Cadillac, a cigar and a ticket to the bullfights" (Krauze 1998: 460, 543).

As we saw in chapter 2, the Mexican middle class thrived during the Growth Era, seizing the opportunities offered by expansion of the economy, the educational system, and state employment. Between 1940 and 1980, the middle class proportion of the population tripled and middle-class incomes rose impressively. Middle-class Mexicans had other reasons to be pleased. Church-state relations continued to improve, with encouragement from Cárdenas's successor, Manuel Avila Camacho, who famously declared, "I am a believer" (Krauze 1998: 506). The pubic school curriculum assumed a blander ideological tone, and the state became more supportive of private education.

The middle class was also favored by a shift in political rhetoric. By 1950, the PRI had abandoned the language of class struggle and adopted the middle class as an "ideal." An official party declaration observed that the "participation of the middle classes in the history of Mexico has been consistently and decidedly helpful in bringing to realization social benefits of major magnitude" (Cline 1967: 326). Clearly, the middle class embodied the urban, educated, industrial—in short, modern—Mexico that the country's rulers dreamed of. It had become, in effect, the "vanguard" class of the Revolution, its raison d'etre (Loaeza 1988: 130).

Within the party, the middle class was represented by the CNOP (National Confederation of Popular Organizations). Launched in 1943, the CNOP was an arbitrary assemblage of organized social sectors—preeminently state bureaucrats and teachers, but also small businessmen, professionals, farmers, youth, women, and others. Middle-class support for Almazán's opposition candidacy in 1940 certainly provided some of the impetus for the new organization. The intraparty discussions leading to its establishment had focused on the marginalization of the middle class within a party structure dominated by worker and peasant organizations. Formally their coequal in a new trilateral structure, the CNOP became the dominant sector of the party. Its influence was reflected in the prominence of CNOP leaders in party positions and public office and in the benefits lavished on an important sector of the middle class: civil servants (Loaeza 1988: 141–44; Knight 1991: 308–9).

But however much the middle class was glorified by the party, privileged within its ranks, and favored by economic policy, this Mexican vanguard class had no more political power than its proletarian counterparts in communist states. The response to the challenge represented by Almazán was revealing: the party imposed its own moderate candidate as successor to Cárdenas. The regime could be responsive where matters of ideology or policy were concerned, but it would be inflexible when power was at stake. Beyond the narrow confines of the tamed electoral arena and the hidden internal party debate, there was little space to challenge the regime or its policies. Occasionally, some middle-class interest group would defy the authorities, almost always in vain. Striking teachers, pilots, and doctors evoked harsh responses from the government. A national strike of government doctors in 1965 ended with the military occupation of a Mexico City hospital and dismissals and arrests of physicians.

The most significant middle-class movement of this period emerged in response to the government's Free-Text Program, launched in 1960 to create and distribute primary school textbooks. The new texts were to be "free, universal, and mandatory." They were, in other words, to be given to every child without charge and used without exception in every school—public or private, Catholic or secular. In a country where most children could not afford textbooks, this was an important and popular innovation. But many middle-class Mexicans saw the Free-Text Program as a plan to indoctrinate their children by, for example, imposing an official version of Mexican history. The program was especially troubling to middle-class parents who had placed their children in Catholic schools to escape the regime's influence.

A surprisingly diverse, but largely middle-class, protest movement developed around the free text issue, centered in conservative provincial cities such as Monterrey, Puebla, and Guadalajara. It drew support from private school, business, and Catholic organizations, encouraged by the Church and by PAN, the conservative opposition party. The movement climaxed on February 2, 1962, in a still famous demonstration in the northern industrial city of Monterrey, which drew 100,000 to 300,000 protestors.

The government was unyielding on the principles of "mandatory and universal," though authorities did mollify some opponents of the free texts by allowing that private schools were free to use other books in combination with the official texts. But when a committee of Monterrey free-text activists visited the city of San Luis Potosí, they were arrested and held without explanation for several days. For both sides, power was at stake, as much as, if not more than, policy. The partisans of private schools wanted unimpeded control over the education of their children. The regime could not tolerate the consolidation of a national, middle-class protest movement. Gradually, support for the anti–free-text movement dissipated, both because of official intransigence and because some participants, notably business leaders and the Catholic bishops, had other pressing issues they hoped to resolve privately with the government (Loaeza 1988: 179–408; Gilbert 1997: 288–89).

Gabriela Meléndez, who studied in Catholic schools during this period, remembers having two sets of textbooks, one Catholic, the other official. The official texts were not used, but were kept on hand in case an inspector arrived from the education ministry. Gabriela and her classmates were trained to switch textbooks and swiftly remove the crucifixes and saints' images from the walls in such an emergency. The drill must have made a strong impression on young minds, but, as she recalls, the inspector never came.

Although the anti–free-text movement drew energy from a cadre of militant Catholics, the controversy should not be interpreted as the rekindling of the conflict between a staunchly pro-Church middle class and an anticlerical regime that the country had suffered in the 1920s and 1930s. The government had no interest in provoking the Catholic Church. But more subtle forces were eroding the traditional hold of the Church on the middle class. As Mexico modernized, the Church was forced to compete for middle-class minds with the radio, television, movies, advertising, the universities, the state, and other propagators of new ideas and new models of conduct. A flourishing consumer culture promoted by American companies was redefining middle-class lifestyles.

A national survey from this period (the Civic Culture study, discussed in greater detail below) asked Mexicans to name people they especially admired. The largest single category of individuals mentioned by middle-class respondents was political leaders, followed by entertainers and cultural figures, such as writers and artists. Together these three categories drew two-thirds of all responses. Religious leaders accounted for only 4 percent of responses. In the same survey, 40 percent of middle-class respondents indicated that they did not attend church regularly. Middle-class people were, in fact, less likely to attend regularly than other Mexicans. Another finding from the survey is relevant to middle-class participation in the free-text movement: nearly a third of middle-class respondents had attended a religious (presumably Catholic) primary school; an additional 12 percent had attended a secular private school. These figures, which are significantly higher than comparable contemporary statistics, suggest why many felt they had a stake in the issue. But their concerns may have centered on education, as much as or more than on religion (Civic Culture-1959).

Loyal, Passive, and Cynical

Until the late 1980s, elections in Mexico could hardly be described as contests for power. PAN, the only significant opposition party, was lucky to break into double digits in national balloting. For the PRI, elections presented an opportunity to mobilize its support, with the help of the tightly controlled labor and peasant organizations, and legitimize its rule.

In the absence of both competitive elections and exit polling, there is no easy way to gauge political opinion during this period. But we can learn something about middle-class attitudes toward the regime from the social science research of the era, beginning with Almond and Verba's Civic Culture survey conducted in 1959, the midpoint in the Growth Era. The survey was part of a five-nation study of political culture, which did not especially focus on social class and was limited, in Mexico, to the urban population in cities over 10,000 (Almond and Verba 1963). For this book, I have reanalyzed the original Civic Culture data to explore class differences. The exclusion of the rural 60 percent of the population does not present a problem for gauging the attitudes of the largely urban middle class, though the only comparisons that can be made are with the urban popular classes.

The Civic Culture data suggest broad middle-class support for the post-revolutionary regime. They show, for example, that a decisive majority of middle-class Mexicans voted for the PRI in the 1958 national elections (table 5.1). Relatively few failed to vote and very few voted for the opposition PAN. These findings are, of course, based on self-reported behavior in a political system dominated by a single party. But the survey provides further evidence of middle-class

TABLE 5.1 Political attitudes in 1959 (in percent)

	Middle class	Other urban
Voted in 1958	77	67
Voted for PRI*	85	84
Voted for PAN*	11	12
Pride in political or economic system	53	52
Positive goals of revolution	81	63
Goals realized or being realized**	82	83
Expect personal economic gains	78	60
PRI member/supporter	17	22
PAN member/supporter	2	1
Percent agree		
Voters run country	50	69
Minority runs country	80	84
People like me, no say	67	78
Treatment by officials		
Equal	60	38
Serious consideration	26	11

Source: Author's analysis of Civic Culture–1959 data
*Among those who voted
**Excludes those who could not name goals

loyalty to the post-revolutionary regime. Asked an open-ended question about what made them proud of their country, a few middle-class Mexicans mentioned natural beauty, national character, or culture, but more than half referred specifically to the political system and/or the national economy. Asked to specify the goals of the Mexican Revolution, over 80 percent of middle-class respondents spontaneously named positive goals such as economic growth, liberty, and agrarian reform and said that these goals had been or were being realized. Very few characterized the goals of the Revolution negatively or thought that the goals had been "forgotten." These middle-class respondents were also optimistic about their own prospects. Nearly

80 percent expected their families to be better off economically in ten years. Compared to other urban Mexicans at the time, they were more optimistic and more likely to give the regime the implicit validation it needed by participating in elections. They were also more attentive to and knowledgeable about politics.

But the survey also uncovered a deep vein of middle-class cynicism about national political institutions. Half of the middle-class people interviewed were skeptical of the notion that voter preferences were the main determinant of national policy. Strong majorities agreed that the country was run by a few who ignore the interests of the many and that "people like me" have no say. Very few middle-class Mexicans were willing to describe themselves as members of the PRI or even "supporters" of the party. Their expectations about how they might be treated by government officials were almost as bleak as those of less privileged respondents. Sixty percent of middle-class Mexicans thought they would be treated "equally" if they went to a government office with a problem—equally bad, it appears, since very few were convinced their views would receive "serious consideration" by officials.

The discontinuities in the political opinions of middle-class Mexicans were richly illustrated by the views of a forty-year-old technician interviewed for the study. "Sr. C" was optimistic about the future because of "the progress of science in the world and . . . the progress of our country." He believed his children would be even more successful than he had been because educational opportunities were expanding in Mexico. Sr. C. identified with the Revolution, which, he said, grew out of a revolt against the "landlords and the rich" by the victims of "abuses and slavery." His special hero was President Lázaro Cárdenas. He loyally supported the PRI because it "stands for . . . the ideals of the Revolution," but he was not inclined to idealize the ruling party. "Of all the bad [parties]," thought Sr. C., "the least bad one is the PRI." There were ample "reasons for discouragement for those of us who have hopes for our country." The government was corrupt and mismanaged public affairs. The counting of the popular vote was "fraudulent." Politics, he sadly concluded, is not about "justice and equality," but "the ambitions for power" (Almond and Verba 1963: 420–23).

In the mid-1960s, Fagen and Tuohy (1972) surveyed political attitudes in Jalapa, a fast-growing town of about 100,000 near the gulf
coast. They describe Jalapa as a "depoliticized community," characterized by low political participation and considerable cynicism
about politics and politicians. But people in Jalapa were, by and large,
accepting of an authoritarian political system. Most felt that Mexico
and they personally were progressing, both economically and so-
cially. Within this context, people at higher class levels shared the
general cynicism about the political system, but had higher levels of
satisfaction with the status quo, higher levels of political participation, and a stronger sense of personal political efficacy. These generalizations apply especially to their top class—labeled "upper class" but
including most of the people whom I have been describing as middle
class. Based on membership in a political party, almost always the
PRI, contacts with officials, and participation in other political activities, the researchers classified 36 percent of this class as "politically
advantaged," compared with 13 percent in the bottom half of the
population (Fagen and Tuohy 1972: 94).

This contradictory mix of diffuse support for the regime and
cynicism about its workings, evident in the Civic Culture data and the
Jalapa study, has often been observed in research on Mexican political
culture. Kahl (1968: 114–19), who studied working and middle-class
men in the early 1960s, writes of the prototypical "Ambivalent Mexican," who believes that the Revolution had brought real social and
economic "progress" to Mexico but is contemptuous of the "corrupt"
self-serving men who run the country, from national politicians to
local union officials. The factory supervisor whom he quotes at
length could easily be mistaken for Almond and Verba's "Sr. C."
Ambivalent Mexicans, Kahl found, were common at all class levels.

Taken together, these studies describe a population that was, as I
suggested at the beginning of this chapter, at once loyal, cynical, and
passive in its orientation toward the post-revolutionary regime. The
middle class shared this general profile with the urban popular majority. On the other hand, middle-class people tended to be more
politically aware, active, and connected. They placed greater value on
democracy. By and large, these differences were of little importance,
except to the extent that they conferred an advantage in dealing with

the authorities over private matters. Over time, they would assume broader significance, beginning with the dramatic events of 1968.

Tlatelolco, 1968

During the summer of 1968, a broad-based, anti-authoritarian, pro-democratic youth movement flowered in Mexico City. Most of the participants were middle-class university and preparatory students who had grown up in the miracle years.[1] In the 1960s, they had ample exposure to the Mexican version of the international youth culture of the era and to the radical ideals of the Cuban revolution. The protestors ranged from political naifs to party militants of all stripes, though many of the leaders were drawn from the organized Left.

At its height in August, the movement was able to attract hundreds of thousands of protestors to the Zócalo, the city's historic central plaza. Although largely peaceful, the student-led marches and meetings had evoked an increasingly violent official response. To get at striking high school students holed up in the San Ildefonso Preparatory School, soldiers fired a bazooka through the school's massive eighteenth-century carved wooden doors, and then rushed in to beat cowering students and teachers. The capital's two major university campuses, centers of protest organizing, were occupied by military forces backed by tanks. The regime was obviously determined to impose order in advance of the International Olympic Games, which were scheduled to open in Mexico City on October 12.[2]

The movement's bloody denouement was played out the afternoon of October 2, in Tlatelolco, a modest middle-class neighborhood not far from the Zócalo. Residents watched from surrounding high-rise apartment buildings as government forces fired on several thousand demonstrators who had gathered for a meeting in the plaza below. What they saw was not a spontaneous response to provocation, but a coordinated military assault, involving machine guns, helicopters, armored vehicles, and tanks and clearly designed to trap and kill protestors. Later, armed men forced their way into many apartments searching for protestors.

Hundreds were murdered that day. The exact death toll can never be known, because the military removed and disposed of many of the bodies. They also attempted, not entirely successfully, to cleanse the blood-soaked plaza. Thousands of protestors were arrested, beaten, and tortured. Some survivors would spend years in prison.

Among those who came to Tlatelolco on that afternoon was Miguel Arroyo, today a physician and the director of a large medical organization in Cuernavaca. In 1968, he was a second-year medical student at the national university, twenty years old, and, as he recalls, a political innocent. Like many of his classmates, Arroyo was angered by official violence against students that summer and especially by the attack on San Ildefonso. He was soon swept into the protest movement and immersed in an exhilarating world of manic, youthful activity. UNAM was on strike. Arroyo's time was consumed by endless meetings, marches, and demonstrations. He had lodgings near the university, but began to sleep on campus. By challenging the regime, Arroyo and his companions felt that they were doing something monumental, "something without precedent." They were fighting for "political liberty." On the street, they found their cause was popular. "We always felt supported and protected by the people."

At the medical school, striking students elected leaders, organized themselves into "brigades," and sent representatives to a "National Strike Committee." Arroyo joined a small brigade of medical students who went to public markets and schools to explain the protests. They collected money in the street to pay for printing leaflets. One member of the group whom Arroyo remembers well was a sweet, sensitive, pretty student from Oaxaca, with a talent for languages. She translated their leaflets into English and other languages so the brigade could distribute them to foreign visitors.

When the shooting began on October 2, Arroyo was close to the Chihuahua apartment building, where speakers were addressing the gathering from the second story. The attackers fired on the protestors from the Chihuahua and from the rear of the crowd. Arroyo heard machine fire sweeping the plaza and saw blood on the ground. He managed to find refuge in a ground-level store in the building. As he remembers it, the shooting went on for perhaps forty minutes. Then he heard boots. Soldiers were hosing down the plaza. "I saw them throwing bodies of the dead into trucks. It was like the Nazis with the Jews. I couldn't believe that this was happening. It was as if I were dreaming it."

Arroyo was discovered in his hiding place, beaten, and jammed into a van with other survivors. As they proceeded out of town in a military caravan at about 1 a.m., he heard a voice outside scream, "*Asasinos, a donde los llevan?*" (Murderers, where are you taking them?). Someone replied from the van with rifle fire. For some reason, after all that had happened, Arroyo found this especially terrifying.

Arroyo was held at the soon to be infamous Campo Militar #1. One day, he says, guards "pointed to a smoking chimney and told us bodies were being burned and we would be next." But after about a week, Arroyo was released with a group of some 500 prisoners. An officer addressed them, saying, "'You are being liberated thanks of the generosity of President Díaz Ordaz.' He made us applaud the president."

Having had no news of their friend with the talent for languages, someone in Arroyo's brigade called her parents in Oaxaca. They learned that she had been at home on October 2 and wanted to return to the capital to see what had become of her companions. When her parents barred her from going, she shut herself in her room and committed suicide after writing notes to her parents and fellow briga-distas blaming President Gustavo Díaz Ordaz.

In 1970, Arroyo voted for the first time, in the small town just outside Cuernavaca where he had grown up and where his father, a teacher and justice of the peace, was well known. At the polling place, he took the paper ballots for the lesser offices and tore them into small pieces in front of election officials. On the presidential ballot he scrawled a message about the PRI's presidential candidate: "Instead of running for president, Echeverría should be on trial for murder." (It was and is widely believed that Luis Echeverría, as interior minister, had orchestrated the Tlatelolco massacre for Díaz Ordaz.) Arroyo would not vote again until the mid-1980s.

"I did not let the experience [of 1968] embitter my life," says Arroyo, "but I never forgot." He would share his memories of the movement and Tlatelolco with successive cohorts of the medical students he trained.

Relatively few middle-class Cuernavacans participated in the 1968 movement, if only because they were not of the right age or did not study in Mexico City, but many were touched by the movement in one way or another. Lili Arce, a middle-class Cuernavaca housewife ten years older than most of the students, had a disturbing conversation that summer with her brother-in-law, a civil servant employed in the Palacio Nacional. On the day of their conversation, he had been ordered to the Zócalo to participate in a pro-government counter-demonstration. There he had seen student protestors crushed by tanks. Like her brother-in-law, Arce was shocked, but when she suggested that the incident would surely be reported on the evening news and in the morning papers, he laughed at her naiveté: "*Estas loca?* It will never be mentioned." That moment radically altered her view of the regime.

Jorge Salazar, Patricia Ramirez, and Angela Picón, later residents of Cuernavaca, were living in Mexico City in 1968. Salazar supervised truck drivers at the health ministry, one of whom also worked part-time driving a sanitation truck for the city. The night of the massacre, he later told Salazar, he had been pressed into service to drive his truck from Tlatelolco, where soldiers loaded it with bodies, to Campo Militar #1, where they were unloaded. Ramirez, who would one day teach in Cuernavaca schools, heard frightening accounts of October 2 from two Tlatelolco residents who worked in her office. Government agents had invaded their apartments searching for students. About the same time, fourteen-year-old Angela was visiting preparatory schools she might attend in Mexico City with her father. At the Normal, both were shaken by a display of October 2 photographs that unambiguously depicted a massacre. Later her prep school algebra teacher told his students that he had witnessed executions as a soldier at Campo Militar #1.

Julio Bernal, the Cuernavaca schoolboy who wanted to "be somebody," was finishing prep school in 1968 and just becoming aware of politics. The following year, his first at the UNAM medical school, he participated in a commemorative march on October 2. The marchers were attacked by police and Bernal was beaten with a rifle butt. It would be his last pubic protest, but it sealed his opinion of the post-revolutionary regime. His views provoked a bitter argument with his parents about the Tri-color, the name often applied to the PRI because it uses the three colors of the Mexican flag. "My mother and father thought that if we didn't vote for the Tri-color, we would be voting against the country. We had to vote for the flag." His parents expected little from the government, but had another, very concrete reason for their allegiance, the fear, not uncommon in their generation, of violent upheaval. Bernal's peasant grandparents had suffered greatly during the 1910 revolution. "[My parents] said that without the PRI there would be another revolution." Bernal concluded, as he later explained, that the rule of the PRI "would only end when our parents and their generation died."

An event comparable to Tlatelolco in the United States would involve the systematic murder of hundreds of protesting Harvard, Columbia, M.I.T, Chicago, Michigan, and Berkeley students by federal forces in Washington, a few blocks from the White House. Higher education, like many aspects of Mexican society, is centered in Mexico City, home to the nation's most prestigious educational institutions and a large part of its university population. Tens of thousands of middle-class and soon-to-be-middle-class students participated in the pro-democracy movement. Few could have imagined that the government would respond so ruthlessly and that it could do so, as it turned out, with perfect impunity. Like Miguel Arroyo, they would not forget.

There is no way of knowing how most middle-class Mexicans viewed the government's action at the time of the Tlatelolco massacre. They were, of course, dependent on mass media little inclined to offend the regime with candid reporting. Later, many would read Elena Poniatowska's powerful indictment, *La Noche de Tlatelolco* (1971), and see the feature film *Rojo Amanecer* (1989), a terrifying account of October 2 through the eyes of a fictional middle-class family living in the Chihuahua building. What is certain is that the government had alienated many of the leaders of a rising generation of professionals, teachers, businesspeople, journalists, and politicians, whose influence would ripple through the Mexican middle class for years to come.

CHAPTER 6

After Tlatelolco

In the early 1970s, the PRI seemed haunted by the political ghost of Tlatelolco. In his often reprinted book, *El Desafío de la Clase Media* (*The Challenge of the Middle Class*; 1971), Francisco López Cámara, an academic with ties to the party, referred frequently, if obliquely, to Tlatelolco ("that which occurred in 1968"). Presidential candidate López Portillo was more explicit in the 1975 speech quoted earlier, when he spoke of "the crisis of conscience of 1968, . . . the crisis of conscience of the middle class" (López Portillo 1988). For the men of the PRI, the crisis was not moral but political: a crisis of middle-class loyalty to the post-revolutionary regime. This concern, larger than Tlatelolco, motivated the 1975 party conference on the middle class.

Anxious about the rebellion of middle-class youth, party leaders were also troubled by signs of growing middle-class support for the PAN. During this period, López Cámara, who had privileged access to official election data, examined election trends in some predominantly middle-class districts. He concluded that the vote for PAN congressional candidates in such districts in the state of Jalisco rose from 23 percent in 1967 to 37 percent in 1973; in the state of Mexico, from 14 to 32 percent; and, most remarkably, in the state of Puebla, from 18 to 54 percent over the same period. These same districts registered corresponding declines in support for PRI candidates. Allowing for the presence of some non-middle-class electors in middle-class districts, López Cámara (who offers few details about his data or methods), estimated that PAN had received almost half of the middle-class vote nationally in 1973. These findings, which were not published until 1988 but were presumably known to party leaders at the time, seem extravagant. As we will see below, middle-class support for PAN did not reach such levels until the mid-1990s. But the very existence of López Cámara's analysis is indicative of the regime's growing concern about middle-class disaffection (López Cámara 1988: 40–41).

Transitions and Disasters

The regime would manage, until 2000, to maintain its continuity (while avoiding the trap of a personal dictatorship) with the help of the ritual that compelled each president to select his own replacement after serving a single term. But Mexicans learned to dread the transitions between *sexenios*—the six-year presidential periods. Some political or economic disaster always seemed to attend the transfer of power. The 1970 transition was overshadowed by the oppressive memory of Tlatelolco. As if to assure that Mexicans would not forget the bloody lesson of October 2, outgoing president Gustavo Díaz Ordaz bestowed the presidency on Interior Minister Echeverría. Thereafter, a long series of sexenial-ending crises steadily eroded the regime's political legitimacy and public confidence in its capacity to manage the economy, especially among middle-class Mexicans.

1976

A divided PAN did not even bother to contest the 1976 presidential elections, leaving López Portillo with over 90 percent of the vote but not even the illusion of a democratic mandate. Before he could take office, the country was plunged into economic crisis—the inevitable result of six years of reckless government spending supported by foreign loans. Outgoing president Echeverría was forced to devalue the peso. In a fit of anger at the uncooperative private sector, he expropriated large tracts of valuable farmland in the northwest, a gesture that only magnified the crisis. The country had to adopt a stringent economic austerity program approved by the International Monetary Fund (IMF).

But López Portillo and Mexico won an economic reprieve. The confirmation of large petroleum reserves off Mexico's gulf coast early in his presidency had permitted López Portillo to borrow abroad and spend at home on a scale that far surpassed the wanton ways of the previous administration.[1] He borrowed to build up petroleum infrastructure, finance social programs, and expand government ownership of the economy. With oil prices at historic highs and so-called petrodóllars flooding the international financial system, major banks were happy to make big loans to countries with proven petroleum reserves.

1982

For much of López Portillo's period in office, the country lived the giddy pleasures of an economic boom, but in 1982, oil prices collapsed and interest rates soared. Caught in an economic trap, Mexico was unable to service its colossal foreign debt. The 1982 sexenial transition reproduced the 1976 crisis on a grander scale. Again the bad news broke after the election of a new president (Miguel de la Madrid) but before he assumed office. López Portillo, like Echeverría before him, was forced to devalue the currency and accept a punishing set of IMF-approved austerity measures. Not to be outdone by Echeverría's impetuous land expropriations, López Portillo compounded the economic catastrophe he had created by nationalizing the entire banking system as he left office. (This sweeping measure, on the initiative of one man, is evidence of the near limitless power of the presidency at the height of the post-revolutionary regime.) There would be no economic reprieve in 1982. Mexicans would pay dearly for the pleasures of the petroleum boom years.

1985

As de la Madrid struggled with the ruined economy he had inherited, the country suffered another disaster, this one natural, but with serious political consequences. On the morning of September 19, 1985, Mexico City suffered the worst earthquake in the nation's history. Hundreds of buildings collapsed and thousands of people died. A second quake the next day added to the devastation, which was concentrated in areas near the historic center of the city. Among the worst hit were the middle-class neighborhoods of Tlatelolco, site of the 1968 massacre, and the more affluent Colonia Roma. The government's initial response to the catastrophe was slow, inept, and arrogant. In an early statement, President Miguel de la Madrid asserted, in the face of chaos, that the city was returning to normal and that Mexico had no need of foreign help, positions he would soon have to abandon. Too often, government response to pleas for help reflected the bureaucracy's worst habits: officials denied responsibility, stalled (see me next week), awaited instructions from above, or even demanded bribes. Troops sent to the affected neighborhoods did not join in rescue efforts, but obstructed the work of volunteers and looted abandoned homes. The colossal apparatus of the PRI and its affiliated mass organizations, capable of mobilizing thousands for political purposes, never reacted to the emergency.

In bright contrast to the complacency of officialdom, volunteers from neighborhoods across the city sprang into action. Prominent among them were middle-class students from the same campuses that fueled the 1968 protest movement. Individual volunteers and, soon, volunteer "brigades" joined residents digging through the ruins in search of survivors. Special heroes were the "moles," slim young men who navigated narrow passageways into collapsed structures to retrieve trapped victims. Other brigades turned private vehicles into ambulances, collected contributions, prepared and distributed food, staged tension-relieving entertainment in overcrowded shelters, and provided other needed services to earthquake victims. The government's own aid efforts gradually improved under pressure from a network of militant community groups that emerged in the affected areas.

The two great revelations of the earthquake emergency were the regime's incompetence in the face of disaster and the effectiveness of grassroots organization. The spontaneous, bottom-up quality of the volunteer brigades and community groups was the antithesis of the controlled, top-down character of regime-affiliated groups such as the official unions. Volunteers and community activists displayed a civic spirit that implicitly rebuked the self-serving, often corrupt ways of officialdom. Mexicans, it seemed, were better than their rulers.

Some optimistic opponents of the PRI imagined that the grassroots activity that flourished in the aftermath of the quake would soon develop into a broader challenge to the regime. They were, for the moment, disappointed. But the shared organizational experience of that period encouraged the growth of so-called civil society in

Mexico—independent citizen groups concerned with urban issues, democratic freedoms, human rights, the environment, women's liberation, and other public matters. The activists in this emerging sector would be disproportionately middle-class people, such as the physician Cuauhtémoc Abarca, who became a community leader in Tlatelolco, and Sergio Aguayo, an academic who organized a national network of election observers that would play a vital role in Mexico's democratization.

1988

The next sexenial transition rolled the economic and natural disasters of the 1980s into a crisis of political legitimacy. The country had endured its worst period of economic stagnation in many decades. Faith in the regime had been further undermined by response to the earthquake and revelations of official corruption, especially during the López Portillo years. On election day 1988, early returns suggested that two strong opposition candidates, on the left and right, were drawing much of the vote. It appeared likely that the PRI's Carlos Salinas might be the first of the party's presidential candidates to fall short of a majority and just possible that his opponent on the left, Cuauhtémoc Cárdenas, could actually win. Authorities halted the vote count, claiming, falsely, that the electoral computer system had collapsed. Few Mexicans believed the official results, announced a week later, awarding Carlos Salinas a bare majority (50.4 percent) of the vote. Salinas had already claimed his dubious victory, while acknowledging the obvious: "The era dominated in practice by a single party is ending" (Preston and Dillon 2004: 170–71).

1994

A cinematic version of the sexenio-ending year 1994 might open with the dark music of the shark theme from *Jaws* and close with something akin to the shattering of thousands of dishes flying out of cabinets on the sinking *Titanic*.

There was no good reason to expect such a year. Carlos Salinas had been an unexpectedly effective president, restructuring the economy along neoliberal lines, steering the country into a generally popular trade pact with the United States and Canada, and presiding over a healthy period of economic expansion. Under pressures intensified by the questions surrounding his own election, Salinas had supported electoral reform legislation, and, in July 1994, the official candidate, Ernesto Zedillo, won a convincing victory in strongly contested, carefully monitored elections.

But 1994 also brought a series of revelations that left Mexicans doubting the stability of their society and the regime they had long depended upon. The year opened with the sudden emergence of the Zapatista guerrilla movement in the southern state of Chiapas. Three months later, at the other end of the country, the PRI's popular presidential candidate, Donaldo Colosio, was assassinated in Tijuana. Zedillo, Colosio's replacement, played on the popular fears of social disintegration inflamed by the Chiapas revolt and Colosio's assassination, a strategy that undercut the Cárdenas campaign on the left. But shortly after the elections, José Ruiz Massieu, one of the PRI's top leaders, was murdered as he left a morning meeting in Mexico City. The party itself seemed to be disintegrating.

As he prepared to take office in December, Zedillo learned that he was inheriting another economic disaster. The apparent prosperity of Salinas's last years in office had been maintained by an overvalued currency, a corresponding trade imbalance, and unsustainable short-term borrowing abroad. Zedillo was forced into the now familiar drill: a devaluation followed by commitment to a painful, IMF-certified austerity program. In 1995, the Mexican economy registered a wrenching contraction, and middle-class families suffered the income shock described in earlier chapters.

Engañados

Variants of the verb *engañar* crop up frequently when middle-class Cuernavacans talk about Carlos Salinas and the economic crisis he left behind. *Engañar* means to deceive or betray or, in a marital context, to be unfaithful. "*Nos engañó. Salinas engañó* 80 percent of the population," says an older professional man, who had long supported the PRI. "He had us *engañados,*" concludes a bank manager. "Mexico was going to be a great power. That's what we heard from the newspapers and on TV. But many things were hidden."

In the early 1990s, many middle-class Cuernavacans were capti-
vated by Salinas and his program of economic modernization. They
supported opening Mexico to the global economy and signing the
NAFTA accord. National and international media told them Salinas
was a great statesman and their own rising incomes seemed to confirm his genius. "We were going to become part of the First World,"
recalls a Cuernavaca businessman. "No longer the Third World. The
dollar was controlled. Inflation was down. From the media and inter-
nationally we heard that Salinas was modernizing Mexico. Apparently good." This third sexenial-ending economic crisis had crystal-
lized his wavering feelings about the ruling party. "Echeverría had
done it to us. López Portillo had done it, and now Salinas. Once
again, we Mexicans had been engañados by the PRI."

Draining the Reservoir

In the 1980s and 1990s, rising numbers of middle-class Mexicans, like
millions of their compatriots, were abandoning a regime they had
come to regard as corrupt, high-handed, and incompetent. The old
system of corporatist political control (always weakest for the middle
class) was decaying. The grateful generation of men and women who
had joined an expanding middle class in the 1940s and 1950s was
aging. The traditional bases of legitimacy in the Revolution and the
economic expansion of the Growth Decades were fading, and nothing convincing had been put in their place. At the same time, a
succession of failed presidencies was undermining faith in Mexico's
unique system of serial autocracy.

The threat of mass middle-class desertion had, of course, long
preoccupied PRI strategists. But the post-revolutionary regime had
accumulated a large reservoir of middle-class support during the
Growth Decades, which only gradually drained away. Middle-class
and popular-class Mexicans alike had voted overwhelmingly for the
PRI in 1958, according to the Civic Culture survey (see table 5.1).
As late as 1983, approximately 70 percent of adults in middle-class
occupational categories described themselves in a national poll as
PRI sympathizers; only 15 percent said they were PAN supporters (Basañez 1999: 225).[2] In the more competitive political environment of 1990, a respectable 43 percent of middle-class Mexicans told

interviewers for the World Values Survey that they would vote for the PRI "if there were a national election tomorrow"—a figure equal to the combined proportions of the two main opposition parties, PAN and the leftist PRD (Partido de la Revolución Democrática). But when the question was repeated in the 1995 version of the survey, PRI and PAN were tied among middle-class respondents with about 35 percent each, while PRD trailed with 25 percent (WVS-1990, WVS-1995). In other words, 60 percent were ready to vote for the opposition.

By the July 1994 elections there was little more than fear of the unknown holding many middle-class Mexicans to their traditional political moorings. After the Peso Crisis of December 1994, all that was needed to pull them away was a credible opposition candidate.

Political Culture

Political culture—the broad dispositions toward the political system that distinguish a nation or a social group—is one key to the middle-class abandonment of the post-revolutionary regime. There is ample evidence that, relative to the popular majority, middle-class Mexicans are more attentive to politics, more knowledgeable about government, more likely to participate in political activities, and more confident in the efficacy of participation. They also have greater faith in democracy and reform. It was to be expected that those who hold such attitudes would be the first to turn against a floundering authoritarian regime, like Mexico's in the 1980s and 1990s.

These class differences in political culture develop early in life, according to Rafael Segovia's classic study of political socialization (1975). Segovia surveyed 3,500 ten- to fifteen-year-olds enrolled in Mexican public and private schools (all of whom would, of course, have been of voting age by 2000). He found that the private school students and those whose fathers held upper-white-collar jobs knew more about politics and were more democratic in their attitudes than their less privileged peers. For example, 80 percent of the sons and daughters of professionals and managers, but only 55 percent of the children of workers and peasants, could identify PAN as a national opposition party (Segovia 1975: 39–40).

Class differences among adults are evident in Almond and Verba's

TABLE 6.1 Some class differences in political culture, 2000
(in percent, unless otherwise noted)

	Middle class	Popular
(a) Discuss politics regularly	46	23
(b) Very interested in 2000 presidential campaign	68	47
(c) Can name 3 branches of national government	57	22
(d) Report voting in 2000 elections	96	87
(e) Reject strong leader, free to ignore Congress or elections	50	35
(f) Agree: economy functions poorly in democracy	42	57
(g) Agree: democracies not good at keeping order	44	51
(h) Favor "reform" of society (over revolution or defense of status quo)	62	49
(i) Agree: Most people try to take advantage of you	66	69
(j) Voluntary organization memberships (number per person)	1.4	0.9

Sources: Mexico Panel Study–2000 (a, c), *Reforma/LA Times*–2000 (b), WVS-2000 (d–j)

1959 Civic Culture survey and many subsequent studies of political culture.[3] The middle-class Mexicans polled in 1959 were more likely to talk to others about politics, more likely to know the names of party leaders, more likely to vote (in the 1958 national elections), and more likely to reject the undemocratic notion that "strong leaders" could do more for the country than "laws and talk" (Civic Culture-1959). These differences have persisted over the last half-century. According to three national polls conducted in the 2000 election year, middle-class people are more likely to discuss politics regularly, know the names of the three branches of the national government, vote in national elections, and distrust the idea of a strong leader unchecked by democratic procedures (see table 6.1).[4] They are also more likely to belong to voluntary organizations, a characteristic often associated with a democratic political culture. On the other hand, middle- and popular-class Mexicans exhibit similarly low levels of another characteristic presumed to be associated with democratic traditions, so-called social trust.[5]

In the last chapter, I made a different point about Mexican political culture: for many decades, Mexicans of all classes remained loyal to a regime whose everyday operations they regarded with deep cynicism. This diffuse support was based on the capacity of Mexico's rulers to associate themselves with a revolutionary myth and claim credit for the spectacular economic growth of the postwar period. Unfortunately, recent surveys do not facilitate long-term comparisons on these matters. Contemporary researchers seldom ask people about "the Revolution," perhaps because such questions might mean little to the majority of Mexicans who have no memory of the regime in its early, most radical years. However, a June 1994 survey conducted by researchers at UNAM did ask whether the government should support or change "the ideas of the Mexican Revolution." Preference for change was most common among middle-class respondents (Beltran et al. 1996: 120).[6]

Two different points about political culture are being made here. One is that the developments of the last three decades (along with the passing of generations) have weakened the foundation of Mexico's shared, post-revolutionary political culture. The other is that the more engaged, democratic political culture of middle-class Mexicans opened them to political change in the late 1980s and 1990s. Note that this second proposition does not necessarily depend on shifts in middle-class political culture. It assumes only that elements of political culture long characteristic of middle-class Mexicans predisposed them, under altered national circumstances, to turn against the post-revolutionary regime.

Looking Back

In 2000, Vicente Fox won an unexpected victory over the official candidate with extraordinary middle-class support. According to the exit poll data analyzed in the next chapter, middle-class voters contributed powerfully to the PRI's defeat. In retrospect, it seems that the regime's worst moments made their biggest impressions on middle-class observers. The terrible lessons of the 1968 Tlatelolco massacre and the 1985 earthquake relief operation were burned into the minds of middle-class students and the middle-class residents of the affected neighborhoods. The concentration of educational institutions and students in Mexico City intensified the long-term impact of these episodes. In 1988, the government's manipulation of election returns posed basic questions of political legitimacy, especially troubling to middle-class Mexicans. The economic crises that accompanied the 1976, 1982, and 1994 transitions had a cumulative, negative effect, undermining middle-class confidence in the government's capacity to manage the economy. Among Mexican households, middle-class families probably suffered the greatest proportional economic losses in the 1982–83 downturn, as they certainly did in 1994–95.[7] All these events were interpreted through the lens of a middle-class political culture that was more engaged, more critical, and more open to change.

CHAPTER 7

The July 2000 Elections

On Sunday July 2, 2000, election day in Mexico, I visited two polling places in middle-class neighborhoods of Cuernavaca. The first, in the upper-middle-class *colonia* where I was living, was selected because a friend was a volunteer poll worker there. Actually, she had been more or less drafted for the position, after being chosen randomly from the voter lists by the independent election commission. This method of recruitment was designed to keep any party, especially the official one, from taking over the balloting process. A commission official came to the house to explain what she was supposed to do and left an instruction manual and video. The volunteers were not paid, though lunch was provided.

Election Day

We arrived at the open-air polling place around 8 a.m. Poll workers were still setting up and the voting got started late. But it was obvious that the day had been meticulously planned. For example, the ballot boxes, assembled on the spot, were of clear plastic—insurance against what were known as "pregnant" ballot boxes, pre-stuffed by the PRI operatives for delivery to polling places in many past elections. (The PRI's election "alchemists" were famous for their ability to turn electoral lead into gold.) Neighbors, waiting for the balloting to begin, stood around chatting. The atmosphere, on this sunny Sunday morning, was casual, almost festive, like that of a weekend farmers' market in a comparable American suburban community. At some point, representatives of the election commission stopped by to check on things. Once it began, the balloting was orderly, efficient, and uneventful.

After watching for a while, I moved to another open-air polling place in a neighborhood that could be characterized as lower middle class. Here the balloting was also conducted smoothly and a similarly casual atmosphere prevailed. Again, the proceedings were open to observation by anyone who cared to watch, including an unidentified foreigner. Only the actual marking of ballots by electors, in portable polling booths carefully designed to guarantee privacy, was shielded from public scrutiny.

At 6 o'clock, voting ended and counting began. The ballots were taken from the transparent boxes and opened one by one under the watchful eyes of official party observers and a loose circle of neighbors. A poll worker read each ballot in a disinterested monotone, "PAN, PAN, PRI, PAN, PAN . . ." As he droned on, it quickly became apparent that there were many, many more PAN than PRI or PRD ballots. This was no small matter for a neighborhood that had traditionally voted PRI and was still represented by PRI legislators. But there was no overt reaction from anyone to this unspoken revelation —as if the assembly were holding its collective breath. No sighs, groans, cheers, smiles, or other expressions of satisfaction, disappointment, or amazement. I did notice that the features of the PRI observer's face gradually slackened. A neatly dressed older man, he had been hovering over the ballot reader, but, as the count continued, he slowly dropped back and sank into a chair. He was clearly unprepared for this outcome. When the counting was complete, the tallies for each office, written in large numbers that could be read at a distance, were posted on a nearby wall for all to see.

At a nearby polling place the reactions of another PRI observer were probably less transparent. Julio Bernal, the Cuernavaca schoolboy who wanted "to be somebody," the first-year medical student who demonstrated against the government and then argued bitterly with his parents about the Tri-color, had agreed to serve as a PRI election observer at a friend's request. Bernal's low opinion of the ruling party had not changed, but he had learned to be more discreet about his politics. As he watched the vote count and saw the PAN's enormous advantage, Bernal struggled to hide his emotions. He was thrilled at the PRI's defeat.

By 8:30 that evening the AP was calling the presidential election for Vicente Fox. An hour later, he was being interviewed on Televisa,

Mexico's biggest TV network. He was obviously confident but not claiming victory. Fox was accompanied by his four children, ages twelve to twenty-something, whom he introduced with open paternal pride, describing the accomplishments of each. Remarkably, Fox and the Televisa anchor, addressed one another in the informal *tu*. There was, of course, no established election-night protocol for a live interview with a victorious opposition presidential candidate. At eleven sharp, as promised, the head of the electoral commission announced the official results. Seconds later, President Zedillo appeared from Los Pinos, the presidential palace, in front of an outsized portrait of Benito Juárez, a nineteenth-century president and national hero, whom Mexicans remember as a champion of democracy. With uncharacteristic eloquence and grace, Zedillo congratulated Fox on his victory and promised his cooperation in the transition to a new administration. He emphasized, as if to foreclose any contrary claims from his own party, that Fox would be president of Mexico in December. Many PRIistas would never forgive him.

That night, Dr. Miguel Arroyo, veteran of the 1968 student movement and survivor of the Tlatelolco massacre, was among the celebrants in Cuernavaca's main plaza. Arroyo had become a PAN activist. In the plaza, he saw one of his companions from 1968 who had, he knew, been active in leftist politics. Smiling, the man yelled, "*Afuera asasinos!*"

The Eyes of a Snake

Middle-class Cuernavaca was delighted with the outcome of the election. A college student who joined his parents in voting for Fox thought that the ruling party had gotten what it deserved, "after all they have done. They were always crooks (*rateros*). I've seen it," he said. "I've read about them. I've listened to my parents and grandparents." He blamed the regime for his middle-class family's economic problems in recent years. Ironically, a classmate, also from a middle-class Cuernavaca family, whose father was a PRI official, did not even bother to vote. She describes herself as apolitical.

In conversations in the months before and after the 2000 elections, three-quarters of my Cuernavaca respondents who expressed an opinion indicated that they would vote for or had voted for the PAN candidate. But their support was based on antipathy toward the PRI, not loyalty to the PAN or enthusiasm for Fox, whom many described as "coarse" (*ranchote*) or "vulgar." Some shared the modest hope that the PANistas would be "less crooked" than the alternative, but none appeared ideologically drawn to PANismo. A government scientist indicated that she intended to vote against the PRI and for the candidate "whom I least dislike," probably Fox. Another woman said she would vote for Fox because there was little hope for Mexico under the continued rule of the PRI. She described the official candidate, Francisco Labastida, as having the "eyes of a snake." A merchant with long-standing leftist inclinations reported that he had cast a carefully calculated vote for Fox as the man with the best chance to "finish off the system." Like many Mexicans, but in higher proportions, these middle-class men and women were voting against "the system" and for change, a sentiment skillfully exploited by the Fox campaign.

Fox would be, for many middle-class Cuernavacans, a disappointing president. But the larger, enduring victory belonged to the nation. That Sunday, Mexicans had ratified a peaceful transition from one-party rule and serial autocracy to a multiparty democracy. Mexico's independent election authorities had won the confidence of voters and outsmarted the alchemists. They had conducted elections as trustworthy and transparent as those clear plastic ballot boxes—an accomplishment that seems even greater in the light of the equivocal outcome of the U.S. elections a few months later.

The Middle-Class Vote

Nationally, as recently as the 1994 presidential election, the PAN and PRI candidates tied among middle-class voters. But in 2000, Fox won 58 percent of the middle-class vote, 32 percent more than Labastida, according to the analysis of data from the *Reforma/LA Times* exit poll presented in table 7.1. This time the two parties were tied among the popular majority.[1] Analysis of a smaller sample from the Mexico 2000 Panel Survey produced similar results.[2] The implication of these figures is that the lopsided vote of the middle-class minority contributed powerfully, perhaps decisively, to the PRI's defeat.

TABLE 7.1 Party preference in presidential elections, by class
(in percent)

Party preference	2000		1994	
	Middle	Popular	Middle	Popular
PRI	26.6	39.0	39.4	54.7
PAN	58.2	40.4	40.3	24.1
PRD	10.9	18.2	18.5	20.1
Others	4.3	2.4	1.8	1.2
Total	100.0	100.0	100.0	100.0
	(n = 347)	(n = 1,679)	(n = 292)	(n = 1,192)

Source: Author's analysis of *Reforma/LA Times*–2000 data
Note: 1994 figures represent retrospective data collected in 2000. Percentages have been rounded and may not total exactly 100.

Within-Class and Between-Class Differences

The middle-class vote in 2000 was remarkably consistent, as can be seen in table 7.2, which refers solely to the middle-class electorate. Differences among middle-class voters by region, education, sex, age, and other relevant variables were modest. For example, region, often a powerful force in Mexican politics, was a relatively weak influence among middle-class electors. Fox carried 60 percent of middle-class voters in the north and 56 percent in the south. Although younger voters have been more open to political change in recent years, the middle class was not divided by a generation gap in 2000. The Cuernavaca college student quoted above, who shared his parents and grandparents low opinions of the PRI, was apparently typical.

Though within-class differences were slim, between-class differences were substantial and pervasive (table 7.3). In the north, PAN's traditional geographic base, middle-class voters were 15 percent more likely to vote for Fox than popular-class voters were. In the south, long a PRI stronghold, the gap was 17 percent. Even among public employees, there was a 13 percent class gap. Two relatively small popular sectors approached middle-class levels of support for Fox: popular-class voters with higher education or middle-class income levels. For most social categories the difference between classes was 15 to 20 percent.

These two tables taken together tell us that, contrary to some interpretations of Mexican electoral politics, class matters. At least it did in 2000, when the middle class was fairly unified in its support of Fox and a large gulf separated most middle-class voters from the popular majority.

TABLE 7.2 Within-class variation among middle-class voters, 2000
(percent of middle-class voters)

	PAN	PRI	PRD and others	Total
Region				
North	60	27	13	100
Central/West central	58	26	17	100
South	56	28	17	100
Education				
No university	52	34	14	100
1+ years university	60	23	17	100
Age				
Younger than 35 years	61	25	14	100
35 years and older	56	28	16	100
Gender				
Men	59	24	16	100
Women	55	29	16	100
Employment sector*				
Public employee	48	34	18	100
Private employee	64	22	14	100
Self-employed	64	19	17	100

Source: Author's analysis of data from Reforma/LA Times–2000
Note: Percentages have been rounded and may not total exactly 100.
*Only statistically significant results

TABLE 7.3 Between-class differences in vote for Fox in 2000 (percent of middle-class voters for Fox less percent of popular-class voters for Fox*)

Variable	Percent difference
Region	
North	15
Central/West Central	20
South	17
Education	
No university	12
1+ years university	7
Age	
Younger than 35 years	16
35 years and older	9
Gender	
Men	20
Women	16
Employment sector	
Public employee	13
Private employee	16
Self-employed	29
Income	
Middle-class levels	2

Source: Reforma/LA Times–2000
*All differences statistically significant except university education and middle-class income levels

These results are also relevant to the classic question raised in chapter 1: Is the population we lump into the middle class sufficiently homogeneous and differentiated from other classes to be considered a social class? By this one test of political behavior, the 2000 vote, the answer appears to be yes, there is a discrete middle class. A Marxist analysis might anticipate a difference based on "employment sector," but among middle-class voters, there appears to be no difference between private sector employees and the self-employed.[3] Though middle-class public sector employees were more supportive of the regime than their peers in the other employment sector categories, they also gave their largest block of votes to Fox. But the class differences within these same employment sector categories were large (tables 7.2 and 7.3). At this critical juncture, the diversity of the middle class did not outweigh its shared disaffection.

Conclusion

In the 2000 election, Vicente Fox prevailed over Labastida by 32 percent among middle-class voters. The ballots of the remarkably undifferentiated middle-class electorate may well have been decisive for Fox's victory. Without them, the PRI candidate might have won, albeit by a margin so fine as to be—especially in the light of Mexican electoral history—unconvincing and dangerous. With them, Fox had an unambiguous mandate, which Zedillo could compel his party to accept. Whatever the future of Mexican politics, middle-class disaffection had brought the PRI-dominated post-revolutionary regime to its definitive end.

Why did the middle-class voters desert a regime they had unthinkingly supported for decades? We can be fairly certain that the answer has nothing to do with political ideology. There was little ideological distance between the PAN and the PRI, the two main competitors for middle-class voters in the 1990s. In particular, PAN supported the government's neoliberal economic program. Students of recent Mexican elections emphasize that they have not turned on ideology or substantive national issues. If there was an issue in the 2000 election, it was the decades-old rule of the PRI and not any policy question. PAN's winning campaign slogan was simple: "Now! Now is the time for change!" *Ya, ya, ya, es hora de cambio!* or just

"*Ya!*"—a notion most likely to appeal to middle-class voters. (In contrast, the PRI's slogan was *Que el poder sirva a la gente,* a lame mistranslation of "Power to the People," probably suggested by American campaign advisors. Both campaigns had American advisors. Fox either had better ones or knew when to ignore them.)

Three factors explain the rising middle-class disaffection of the late 1980s and 1990s. The first was a class political culture that was more engaged, more democratic, and more open to change. The second was the steady erosion of those elements of the political culture that had long sustained the regime, by the passage of generations and the sometimes tragic failures of successive governments. By the late 1990s, middle-class Mexicans had little faith in the dual myths of the Revolution and the Mexican economic miracle. The third factor, examined in the next chapter, was the collapse of middle-class incomes in 1995.

CHAPTER 8

Mixed Fortunes and
Political Disaffection

In the early years of the new century, after two decades of neoliberal economic policy, middle-class Mexicans were not optimistic about the future of their class. A discouraged young professional captured a common sentiment when he claimed that "the middle class is disappearing. All that's left is the marginal class and people with lots of money." Other middle-class Cuernavacans characterized their class as suffering, cornered, crushed, finished, and extinct. Such sentiments were not unique to Cuernavaca. Reporters for the *New York Times* (2002) and the *Houston Chronicle* (2002) heard much the same from middle-class people they interviewed in Mexico City. "The middle class is falling, falling, falling," asserted one man. "The middle class no longer exists. There's rich and poor," lamented another.[1]

Mexico's modern middle class is a product of the booming economy and the developmentalist state of the Growth Era. For more than four decades, GDP growth rarely dipped below 6 percent, an extraordinary record. The government promoted the growth of the middle class with an economic model based on Import Substitution Industrialization, the expansion of middle and higher education, and a swelling public sector rich in white-collar employment opportunities. A country of isolated rural communities was transformed into a nation of cities, with an economy weighted toward manufacturing, commerce, and other services—all settings favorable to middle-class expansion.

Having abandoned the radical social policies of the 1930s, the post-revolutionary regime measured its success by economic growth and rising social mobility. In 1975, José López Portillo (1988: 119) took pride in claiming the middle class as "the most genuine result of the Mexican Revolution." Perhaps the president-to-be underestimated the role of blind market forces in transforming the class structure. For whatever reasons, in the remarkable period from 1940 to 1980, the middle class tripled in relative size.

But in the 1970s Mexico's economic model was showing signs of weakness. Toward the end of the decade, the economy was kept precariously afloat on a tide of oil revenues and foreign loans that abruptly receded in 1982, leaving the country stranded. In the years of crisis and stagnation that followed, national economic policy shifted away from the inward-looking developmentalism of the Growth Era toward export-driven neoliberalism. Mexico opened itself to the global economy and especially the U.S. economy, while reducing the state's role in domestic markets.

The political bond that had developed between the middle class and the regime during the Growth Era was strained by the 1968 Tlatelolco massacre, the financial debacles of 1976 and 1982, the regime's flawed response to the 1985 Mexico City earthquake, and its flagrant manipulation of the vote count in the 1988 presidential election. Disaffection was encouraged by a middle-class political culture that was drawn to democracy and open to change. But the old loyalty proved remarkably resilient. In the early 1990s, a period of renewed prosperity for middle-class households, the PRI could, the available evidence suggests, still claim more middle-class support than any opposition party. It took the storm of the Peso Crisis and the abrupt collapse of middle-class incomes to finally tear the middle class from its political moorings.

Rising Fortunes and the Income Shock

The shifting fortunes of the Mexican middle class in Neoliberal Era can be charted with successive ENIGH surveys. An analysis of the household surveys from 1984 to 2000 yields four significant and sometimes surprising conclusions: (1) the middle class grew larger during the Neoliberal Era, (2) middle-class incomes fell precipitously in the wake of the Peso Crisis, (3) but rose substantially over the entire Neoliberal period, and (4) the gap between the middle class and the rest of the population widened on income and other indicators.

TABLE 8.1   Middle-class households (as percent of all households)

Year	Relative standard*	Alternative absolute standard**
2000	19.5	19.5
1996	18.0	14.7
1994	18.3	19.4
1992	17.9	18.3
1989	16.1	16.0
1984	16.2	13.5

Sources: ENIGH-1984 to ENIGH-2000
*Relative = Upper-white-collar households with incomes over 1.5 times current household median
**Absolute = Upper-white-collar households with real incomes over 1.5 times the 2000 median

As table 8.1 shows, the first conclusion holds up whether middle-class status is determined by the relative standard used throughout this book or by an alternative, absolute standard, based on a fixed real income threshold. An absolute measure is, of course, more subject to year-to-year economic fluctuations, which are smoothed out by a relative standard. The absolute series, in particular, reflects the economic impact of the 1994–95 crisis. By the relative standard, the middle class portion of the population grew by 3 percent over the sixteen-year period. By either measure, the middle class has not expanded at the pace sustained during the Growth Decades, but even modest expansion during the slow-growth Neoliberal Era is significant.

The ENIGH data confirm that middle-class households experienced what I have described as an income shock in the mid-1990s. Between 1994 and 1996, the (real) median middle-class income plunged 40 percent (table 8.2). The fall represented an abrupt reversal of the upward trend of the preceding decade, making the income shock all the more jolting. But by 2000, middle-class incomes had largely recovered and were well ahead of where they had been in 1984. Another sensitive indicator of middle-class welfare confirms this pattern of gain, loss, and recovery over the Neoliberal period: the number of passenger cars produced annually in Mexico for the domestic market. By the early 1990s, output was double what it had been in

TABLE 8.2 Median monthly household income (in year 2000 pesos)

Year	Middle	Popular	Middle/Popular
2000	12,300	3,200	3.8
1996	8,400	2,600	3.2
1994	13,700	3,700	3.7
1989	10,250	3,350	3.0
1984	8,450	2,950	2.8

Sources: ENIGH-1984 to ENIGH-2000

TABLE 8.3 Passenger car production for the domestic market

Year	Vehicles	Index (1984 = 100)
2000	343,010	171
1999	316,356	158
1998	355,658	177
1997	261,712	131
1996	163,651	82
1995	102,573	51
1994	352,386	176
1992	429,069	214
1988	209,900	105
1984	200,465	100

Source: Motor Vehicle Facts and Figures 1986–2002

1984. Auto production plunged in 1995 but rebounded in the late 1990s (table 8.3).

Additional evidence of the growing prosperity of the middle class can be found in a series of material indicators from the ENIGH surveys, such as vehicle and appliance ownership (table 8.4). While new car sales gauge year-to-year fluctuations in middle-class fortunes, these indicators measure the accumulation of domestic capital over time. By 2000, according to the ENIGH data, swelling majorities of middle-class families had such modern essentials as telephones, automobiles, washing machines, and substantial housing—luxuries that significantly change the character of everyday life.

TABLE 8.4 Material indicators, 1984–2000
(percent of households possessing)

Material goods	1984	1994	2000
Telephone			
Middle	48	69	83
Popular	11	18	30
Difference	*37*	*51*	*53*
Vehicle			
Middle	62	70	80
Popular	13	19	25
Difference	*49*	*51*	*65*
Home with 5+ rooms and modern plumbing			
Middle	65	80	88
Popular	21	31	38
Difference	*44*	*49*	*50*
Washing machine			
Middle	70	83	86
Popular	26	37	49
Difference	*44*	*46*	*37*
Computer			
Middle	—	16	42
Popular	—	1	5
Difference	—	*15*	*37*

Sources: ENIGH-1984, ENIGH-1994, ENIGH-2000
Note: Home standard includes kitchen and bathroom in room count. "Modern plumbing" assumes bathroom and water piped into residence.

As the middle class has grown more affluent, the disparities between it and the popular majority have widened. Popular household incomes have increased during the Neoliberal Era, but only marginally. The median middle-class income has advanced from 2.8 to 3.8 times the popular median since the early 1980s (table 8.2). Class differences in material possessions have also increased for all indicators except washing machines, which can now be found in the majority of Mexican households (table 8.4). Computers, increasingly common in middle-class homes remain quite rare in popular-class households, even those with incomes at middle-class levels.[2]

Education

The Cuernavaca interviews suggest that, during the Neoliberal Era, middle-class families have made an extraordinary commitment to the education of their children, which was, if anything strengthened by the economic misfortunes of the mid-1990s. Most of the school-age children of the families studied were, as we saw in chapter 4, enrolled in private schools. The vast majority of their sons and daughters beyond school age were attending or had attended college.

The ENIGH surveys indicate that the educational gap between the middle and popular classes grew in the Neoliberal Era. Table 8.5 compares the educational attainment of heads of households at two key levels: (1) completion of secundaria or higher and (2) the completion of one or more years of university studies. It appears that Mexicans generally are spending more years in school. But the class disparity has not narrowed at the secundaria level and has grown significantly at the university level. Among young adults there is further evidence of growing educational inequality. In 2000, 70 percent of all seventeen-to twenty-two-year-olds from middle-class households were studying at preparatoria[3] or university-level institutions, compared with 25 percent of their popular-class peers. Because the 1984 ENIGH survey did not ask about current school attendance, similar statistics cannot be generated for that year. But employment data from the surveys reveal a growing class gap in the time available for study. From 1984 to 2000, the proportion of seventeen- to twenty-two-year-olds working twenty hours or more a week rose sharply at popular-class levels but barely changed among middle-class Mexicans (table 8.6).

TABLE 8.5   Educational attainment: heads of households (in percent)

Level of education	Middle	Popular	Difference
Secundaria or higher			
1984	64.1	13.2	*50.9*
2000	84.8	35.2	*49.6*
University, 1 or more years			
1984	38.3	2.7	*35.6*
2000	57.8	5.3	*52.5*

Source: ENIGH-2000

TABLE 8.6   Young adults (17–22 years)
working 20 hours or more per week (in percent)

Year	Middle	Popular	Difference
1984	26.5	38.4	*11.9*
2000	27.4	46.8	*19.4*

Source: ENIGH-2000

The growing middle-class preference for private education presents another widening class gap. From 1984 to 2000, the proportion of primary school students in private institutions grew nationally by more than half, according to official statistics.[4] Middle-class families accounted for most, but not all of this growth. Table 8.7 compares class differences in private school enrollments for 1984 and 2000.[5]

Conclusion

The middle class has fared better in the Neoliberal Era than is commonly believed. By 2000, it was notably bigger, better educated, and more affluent than it was in the early 1980s—trends all the more remarkable given Mexico's uneven economic performance. Middle-class Mexicans had more telephones, more household appliances, more and newer cars, and larger houses than they did two decades earlier. A growing percentage of their children attend private schools. As

TABLE 8.7   Private school attendance of children ages 6–11 years
(in percent)

Year	Middle	Popular	Difference
1984	24.4	1.9	*22.5*
2000	37.1	3.2	*33.9*

Source: ENIGH-2000

the middle class has advanced in the Neoliberal Era, the big material and educational disparities between it and the popular majority have grown bigger.

There is an obvious incongruity between these findings and the deep pessimism about the future of their class expressed by the middle-class men and women quoted at the beginning of this chapter. How can we explain this gap between perceived and measured realities? The key suggested in the Cuernavaca interviews is the disjuncture between the dazzling rise of middle-class incomes in the late 1980s and early 1990s and their stunning collapse in the mid-1990s.

The 1995 income shock woke the middle class as from a dream. During the preceding decade, a golden era that glows ever brighter in memory, middle-class Mexicans accustomed themselves to a steadily improving standard of living. Such luxuries as the second car, the home computer, and distant vacations were increasingly taken for granted. They imagined that Mexico had changed, having liberated itself from the decrepit economic regime of the 1970s and early 1980s, with its regular end-of-the-sexenio crises. But December 1994 cast them back to the collapse of August 1982. "We went to sleep with our feet planted firmly in the first world," a disillusioned housewife told a reporter for the *Rocky Mountain News,* "and we woke up in the Third World" (Adams 1995). My respondents in Cuernavaca expressed similar sentiments. They described themselves as engañados: deceived and betrayed by their rulers.

After December 1994, middle-class Mexicans felt that they would be lucky to preserve what they had. Under enormous financial stress, they were compelled to sacrifice the desirable for the indispensable. They clung to expensive private education in the hope it would provide some security for their children in an uncertain future. It mattered little that their own accumulated wealth and the support of extended families shielded them from the full force of the crisis or that middle-class incomes rebounded in the late 1990s to levels well above those of the early 1980s. Nothing would bring back the innocent pleasures of the dream.

In *La Democracia en México* (1965), written in the middle of the Growth Era, Pablo Gonzalez Casanova puzzled over a very different divergence between perception and reality: popular support for a regime that, objectively, favored a prosperous few and cheated the poor majority. Part of his explanation for this anomaly was the *factor esperanza* (the hope factor)—popular faith in opportunities for individual improvement within the existing socioeconomic order. Turning Gonzalez Casanova's concept on its head, we may speak of a *factor desesperanza*, a failure of hope that colored the views of many middle-class Mexicans at the beginning of the new century. Rooted in the shock of 1995, desesperanza skewed their perception of the present, leaving them impervious to evidence of improvement, and undermined their faith in the luminous future they had beheld until December 1994. In July 2000, desesperanza brought their long-simmering political disaffection to a boil.

The July 2006 Election

Imagine this. A middle-class Mexican leaves the planet in 1976 and returns home thirty years later on election day, July 2, 2006. Though the country looks and sounds familiar, it's strangely different—an alternate Mexico. The president, Vicente Fox, is a member of the PAN, a party which, he recalls, had not even bothered to contest the 1976 elections and had never won more than 15 percent of the vote in a national election. The mayor of Mexico City is affiliated with the left-leaning PRD, a party he has never heard of. He learns from his middle-class friends that the main contenders in the current presidential campaign are the PRD candidate, Andrés Manuel López Obrador, the charismatic former mayor of Mexico City; the PAN candidate, Felipe Calderón, a colorless technocrat and ex-energy minister; and the PRI candidate, Roberto Madrazo, a former governor and party strongman. Most of his middle-class friends say that they will vote for Calderón, but more than a few will vote for López Obrador. He is amazed to discover that none intend to vote for Madrazo, whose party they had all supported in the Mexico he remembers. Nationally, the race has come down to a tight contest between López Obrador and Calderón, and no one really knows who the next president will be. He finds this unsettling. In this altered Mexico, the president cannot impose his own successor—Calderón wasn't even Fox's choice for the party nomination—and he does not control the election machinery, which is now in the hands of an agency independent of the government.

As it turned out, Calderón prevailed over López Obrador in 2006, by fraction of a percentage point. In the weeks after the election, López

TABLE E.1 Party preference in 2006 presidential election, by class (in percent)

Political Party	Middle Class	Popular
PAN	50	34
PRD	32	37
PRI	13	25
Other	5	4
Total	100	100
(N)	(4,963)	(23,035)

Source: Author's analysis of data from Consulta Mitofsky exit poll, July 2, 2006

Obrador and his supporters contested his narrow loss with massive demonstrations and legal action before the new Federal Electoral Tribunal. But the tribunal and, by and large, popular opinion accepted Calderón's victory.

The election turned on the middle-class vote, as the figures in table E.1 indicate.[1] Among the popular majority, López Obrador led Calderón by a convincing margin. A shift in the preferences of just one in twenty middle-class voters would have given the election to the PRD. But middle-class Mexicans had reasons to be happy with PAN-led status quo. The economy was growing at a moderate but gradually accelerating pace, with low inflation. Mexico's international debt was shrinking. Under these conditions, the kind of inter-sexenial economic crisis they had learned to fear under the old regime seemed improbable. New car sales, a dependable indicator of middle-class fortunes, climbed to unprecedented levels during this period. By 2004, car ownership among middle-class households was almost universal, and the proportion with computers had jumped to 60 percent (ENIGH-2004).

Yet, middle-class support for PAN was not unanimous. Calderón took half of the middle-class vote, significantly less than Fox had received in 2000. Only a tiny proportion of middle-class voters backed PRI's Madrazo, but, remarkably, a third voted for López Obrador. Within the middle-class electorate, differences by gender, education, and age were modest, about what they had been in 2000, but regional differences were much larger. In particular, middle-class voters in the affluent north were 16 percent more likely to vote for Calderón than their peers in the impoverished south, where López Obrador drew more middle-class votes. These results are consistent with the conclusions in chapter 7 about Fox's sweeping victory among middle-class voters. In 2000, the middle class did not vote for Fox, for PAN, nor for any ideology but voted against the long rule of the PRI. In 2006, the deflated national power of the PRI freed middle-class Mexicans to vote their regional, ideological, and candidate preferences.

Descriptions of the Surveys

I have used data from eleven national surveys to measure and describe the middle class and gauge its opinions and politics. When tables or statements in the text are based on my own analysis of these surveys, the data source is cited as indicated below. In each case, the date following the hyphen (as in ENIGH-2000) refers to the year in which the survey was conducted. (Publications based on these surveys are listed in the bibliography and cited by author and date of publication.)

Each of the data sets analyzed includes variables that specify family income and the occupation of the head of household or principal income earner. Without this information, middle-class respondents as defined here could not be identified. Inevitably, the relevant income and occupational data were far from perfectly compatible from survey to survey. There were significant differences in the questions used and the ways that answers were categorized. For some surveys the class position of many respondents could not be determined from the data and they were excluded from the analysis. I have indicated below when this was the case for a significant proportion of the sample.

Civic Culture Study (cited as Civic Culture-1959)

I have analyzed the Mexico data from this famous five-nation survey of political culture. The 1,000-case Mexico sample was designed to represent the population residing in cities over 10,000. On the original study, see Almond and Verba 1963 and the collection edited by them (1989). The data and documentation were obtained through the Inter-University Consortium for Political Research (ICPUR).

The ENIGH Surveys (cited as ENIGH-1984, etc.)

Mexico's periodic national household survey, the ENIGH (Encuesta Nacional de Ingresos y Gastos de los Hogares) is the gold standard for household economic data. I have made extensive use of the ENIGH-2000 survey and also drawn on five earlier ENIGH surveys, reaching back to 1984. These compatible surveys are conducted by the Mexican census bureau, INEGI (Instituto Nacional de Estadística, Geografía e Informática), and based on representative national samples, usually about 10,000 households. (The 1984 sample was a little less than 5,000 households.) INEGI collects richly detailed occupational and income data and household demographic data. In appendix C, I have given a detailed explanation of how the middle class was measured using ENIGH data. See INEGI 2001c for further information on the series, including definitions of variables. Many of the ENIGH data sets are available on CD-ROM from INEGI.

La Reforma–Los Angeles Times Exit Poll
(cited as Reforma/LA Times-2000)

This national exit poll was conducted by the newspapers *La Reforma* (Mexico City) and the *Los Angeles Times* on election day July 2, 2000. My analysis is based on 2,068 of 3,380 original cases. I am grateful to Professor Alejandro Moreno and Susan Pinkus of the *Los Angeles Times*, who helped me gain access to the data and provided useful advice for their analysis.

Mexico 2000 Panel Study
(cited as Mexico Panel Study-2000)

This multiple-survey study of the Mexican electorate is based on interviews with 3,600 respondents, conducted from February 7 to July 7, 2000. Unfortunately, class position, as understood here, could not be determined for most respondents. The analysis was limited to 633 cases dawn from the later waves of the panel survey. (For the same reason, the related post-election survey could not be analyzed.) For further information about the study and interpretation of the results, see Domínguez and Lawson 2004. The Mexico 2000 Panel Study investigators have made their data freely available. They ask users to provide the following information: Participants in the study included (in alphabetical order) Miguel Basañez, Roderic Camp, Wayne Cornelius, Jorge Domínguez, Federico Estévez, Joseph Klesner, Chappell Lawson (Principal Investigator), Beatriz Magaloni, James McCann, Alejandro Moreno, Pablo Parás, and Alejandro Poiré. Funding was provided by the National Science Foundation and *Reforma* newspaper.

World Values Surveys (cited as WVS-1995 and WVS-2000)

These two surveys form part of a continuing international project tracking changing values in more than eighty societies. For both 1995 and 2000, the Mexico samples were about 1,500 cases, of which close to three-quarters could be included in my analysis. For description of the project, marginal statistics for each country, and the text of the 2000 questionnaire, see Inglehart et al. 2004. I am grateful to Alejandro Moreno and *La Reforma* for providing the 2000 data set and Mexico version of the questionnaire. The 1995 data set was obtained through the ICPUR.

Cuernavaca and the Cuernavaca Sample

The choice of Cuernavaca as a research site raises an inevitable question: Is it a representative Mexican city—an appropriate place to study the country's middle class? The question is analogous to that posed by Robert Redfield's (1930) and Oscar Lewis's (1951) classic studies of rural life in Tepoztlan, just a few miles down the road. Ultimately, such questions can be answered only by the cumulative evidence of other case studies and national surveys. But Cuernavaca seems like a good place to start studying middle-class Mexico. The city is neither isolated nor idiosyncratic. Firmly within the gravitational field of nearby Mexico City, it is very much part of a national society and economy. The establishment of an industrial park and building of a rapid toll road to Mexico City have tightened its links to the national and global economy.

As I noted in the introduction, more than 40 percent of Cuernavacans were born somewhere else. The city's labor force profile, as described by occupational structure, sectoral distribution, and proportions of employers (*patrones*) and high income earners is typical of Mexican cities (table 1.1). Middle-class Cuernavacans patronize the same, typically middle-class-oriented chain stores as their peers in other cities of central and northern Mexico: Comercial Mexicana, Gigante, Wal-Mart, Sears, Sanborns, and Farmacia de Descuento, among others (ANTAD 1999).[1] My research suggests that their economic lives are swept along by the same treacherous currents that rule most of the nation. Like the middle-class households in successive ENIGH surveys, the Cuernavaca families I interviewed generally prospered in the late 1980s and early 1990s, lost ground in the wake of the 1994 Peso Crisis, and recovered, at least in part, in the late 1990s.

The Cuernavaca interviews, with members of fifty-two families, were conducted from 1999 to 2005. Consistent with the definition of middle class presented in chapter 1, the families interviewed were selected for non-routine white-collar occupations and customary monthly incomes equivalent to 6,000 to 65,000 pesos in 2000. The term *customary* is inserted here because the focus of the analyses in chapters 3 and 4 is the effect of the economic crisis on these households. The results would obviously be misleading if families whose incomes had recently fallen to below middle-class levels were excluded from the sample. Customary income refers to monetary income or the equivalent standard of living over a period of several years. In contrast, the ENIGH household surveys measure income at a virtual instant: the three months preceding the survey. The result is a snapshot image of the middle class, excluding many whose careers, standard of living, and usual income are clearly middle class.

Families were recruited for the study by a variety of methods. Many of the early interviews were with friends, relatives, or commercial contacts of the middle-class family I lived with in Cuernavaca. Soon, I began knocking on doors in our relatively affluent neighborhood and later did the same in two more modest middle-class neighborhoods. (Such cold solicitations were often fruitless, but produced more interviews than I anticipated from an experienced colleague's warning, "You'll never get by the maid.") With permission from local school authorities, I wandered through two public primary schools, asking teachers for interviews. (I was also able to interview a private school teacher.) Snowball and target-of-opportunity contacts yielded additional interviews. That is, I asked respondents to recommend others and sought interviews with people I met through chance encounters in offices and other settings. To insure diversity, I monitored and shaped the accumulating sample. For example, noting lacunae at the lower end of the age structure and in the middle of the middle-class income range, I searched for younger respondents and began working in a neighborhood likely to yield households with middling middle-class incomes.

Selected by non-random methods, the families in the study cannot be considered a statistically representative sample of middle-class Cuernavaca or middle-class Mexico. Given the difficulty of finding people willing to sit for long interviews about potentially sensitive

TABLE B.1 (A–C)   Economic profile of families

A. Family income in pesos/month (%)

Under 10,000	36
10,000–19,000	33
20,000 and above	31
Total	100
	(39)

B. Income earners (%)

Male head only	33
Female head only	14
Dual earners	37
Family business	8
None	8
Total	100
	(51)

C. Occupation of principal provider (%)

Professional	33
Small business owner	21
Teacher	13
Manager	12
Retired	10
Other	12
TOTAL	100
	(52)

Note: Percentages have been rounded and may not total exactly 100.

family and financial matters, I adopted a more modest objective: to assemble a sample varied enough to capture the demographic and economic diversity of the middle class. The profiles in tables B.1 and B.2 suggest some success in this effort.

Among those interviewed, there is ample representation of the four largest middle-class occupational categories: professionals (independent and salaried), merchants, teachers, and managers (private and public). Most of the families had current incomes from 5,000 to 35,000 pesos per month. The exceptions were typically households whose incomes deteriorated severely in the wake of the economic crisis or, at the other extreme, those supported by especially lucrative professional practices and businesses.

The majority of households in the sample depend, at least in part, on income from women's work, either in a family business or separate employment (table B.1b). Predictably, younger women are more likely to have separate careers. Based on the predominant ages of children, the families are distributed across the domestic cycle; over half have children of school or college age. Seventeen percent of the households are headed by single females—half of them young mothers with dependent children (table B.2c).

TABLE B.2 (A–C)   Social profile of families

A. Social class of respondent's parents (%)	
Popular classes	39
Middle class	61
Total	100
	(49)
B. Household type (%)	
Dual head	83
Female head	17
Total	100
	(52)
C. Domestic cycle status (%)	
No children over 5 years	12
School-age children	25
College-age children	31
Post-college-age children	33
Total	100
	(52)

Note: Percentages have been rounded and may not total exactly 100.

Detailed questions about social origins revealed that about 60 percent of respondents grew up in middle-class families (table B.2a), about half attended private schools, and many had middle-class grandparents.[2] But given the transformation of the Mexican economy since the 1940s described in chapter 2, it is not surprising that many respondents have experienced significant upward mobility. Among the almost 40 percent of respondents with popular-class origins were a lawyer, an engineer, and a branch bank manager, all sons of peasants, and two doctors whose parents began their adult lives as peasants and later moved on to modest urban occupations. Others were sons and daughters of blue-collar workers.

Precise comparisons between the Cuernavaca sample and the national middle-class sample from ENIGH-2000 are impossible because of various data incompatibilities. Nonetheless, the two samples appear broadly similar. Their income distributions are quite close. The Cuernavaca sample has similar proportions of teachers and managers but a somewhat larger proportion of professionals. (It is impossible to distinguish all small-business owners in the ENIGH data.) Among the Cuernavaca families there is a slightly larger percentage of female-headed households, but a similar proportion of working wives.

The interviews, covering family history, career experiences, and household economy, ran one to two hours and were typically conducted in the family's home. Where possible I interviewed multiple members of the same household and interviewed some individuals repeatedly over the several years of the project. My respondents included thirty men, eighteen women, and four couples. I have drawn on extensive notes from these interviews throughout the book. They are the basis for the personal narratives and a twenty-variable data set, which is the source of any systematic generalizations about the families (including tables B.1 and B.2) and their experiences (notably in chapters 3 and 4). However, because the research depends on a small, non-random sample, I have generally refrained from citing precise statistics, depending instead on characterizations such as "about a third," "the majority," or "a few."

Notes on Defining and Measuring
the Middle Class

*I conceive of the Mexican middle class as consisting of fami-
lies headed by individuals with non-routine, non-manual occupations, living on incomes comfortably above the popular average
but below the peak of the national pyramid. I particularly have in
mind independent and salaried professionals, managers, teachers, technicians, bureaucrats, and merchants (but not low-level
office workers or retail clerks), with household incomes at least
50 percent higher than the median household income.* (from
chapter 1)

This appendix contains supplemental information on defining and
measuring the middle class. No aspect of this research has provoked more discussion. The basic rationale for the definition above—
emphasizing household units of analysis, occupational distinctions,
and a relative concept of income—was laid out in chapter 1. This
definition is, I believe, reasonable, unambiguous, and, in practice,
illuminating. I have used photographs, statistics, and personal narratives to provide a clear sense of whom it covers. But I would re-
emphasize the point made in chapter 1: there are no correct definitions of middle class, but many useful ones.

Measuring the Middle Class with ENIGH Data

The ENIGH household surveys provide the most detailed and trustworthy data available for measuring and describing the middle class.
A family was considered middle class if the occupation of the household head fell into one of the upper-white-collar (non-routine, non-

manual) categories and household income exceeded 150 percent
of the current ENIGH median for all households. (For reasons explained in chapter 1, no upper limit was placed on incomes.) Analyses
of ENIGH data throughout the book are limited to family households
with heads under sixty-five. This specification removed single person,
non-family, and elderly households, about 20 percent of all households, from consideration. It also sharply reduced the number of
households whose class position could not be determined from the
data, generally because no occupation was specified.

Occupations in the following ENIGH categories were considered
middle class: *funcionarios, profesionales, técnicos, trabajadores de educación, trabajadores de arte, supervisores artesanales e industriales,
jefes en actividades administrativas, comerciantes en establecimientos,
agentes y representantes de ventas* (*de seguros, valores, inmuebles*, etc.),
and *patrones*.

The final category, patrones (employers), unlike funcionarios
(executive or manger), is not strictly an occupational category but a
position in the workplace. Two-thirds of respondents with middle-
class household incomes who are classified as patrones fall into one of
the middle-class occupational categories just listed, such as comerciantes (merchants) or profesionales. Most of the remainder are apparently farmers and other owners of small- to medium-sized enterprises in construction, transportation, and other fields, who would
not be considered middle class without the status of *patron*; they
account for just 6 percent of middle-class households.

The ENIGH surveys are distinguished by complex and exhaustive
income data, including data on non-monetary income, such as the
value of subsistence production. The income concept I have employed is "current monetary income," summed for all family members. I have not followed the practice of some analysts who measure
household income in per capita terms. Applied to this research, a per
capita measure would presumably mean that the middle-class income threshold for a family of six was twice that for a family of three.
Though it is certainly the case that six cannot live as cheaply as three,
a household of six does not require twice as many kitchens, bath-
rooms, washing machines, telephones, automobiles, etc., to maintain
a middle-class living standard. Per capita standards can be misleading. A family of five with an income of 6,000 in year 2000 pesos, for

example, would be poor by some per capita poverty standards, but my own observation of such households suggests that they are far from impoverished. Fortunately, there is relatively little variation in size among middle-class households as defined here. Since I am studying families, there are no households of one. Seventy-two percent of middle-class family households have three to five members, 93 percent have two to six members (ENIGH-2000).

Characteristics of Middle-Class Occupations

The definition of middle-class occupations in terms of non-routine, non-manual work reflects, in part, the influence of research conducted by Melvin Kohn and his associates on class differences in child-rearing practices (Kohn 1969; Kohn and Schooler 1983). The researchers found a typically middle-class pattern of socialization that encourages self-direction and tolerance and a typically working-class pattern that emphasizes conformity to authority. They further established that parental values and child-rearing practices are shaped by the character of a parent's occupation (or, in the case of non-working wives, the husband's occupation). Specifically, they showed that people whose work is (1) with people or data, rather than things, (2) non-repetitive, and (3) independent of close supervision tend to develop a distinct set of values, attitudes, and child-rearing practices revolving around self-direction and tolerance. These three features are notably characteristic of middle-class occupations, as defined here.

The observation in chapter 1 that middle-class occupations are distinguished by relatively high incomes, which tend to rise in the course of a career, is supported by tables C.1 and C.2. Note that the median earnings associated with non-middle-class occupational categories are consistently below those of middle-class categories and remain quite flat during the prime working years from age twenty-five to age fifty-five.

The SALA Series of Class Estimates

The *Statistical Abstract of Latin America* (SALA) has published an important series of analyses of Mexico's class structure (Wilkie and

TABLE C.1   Index of median earnings by occupation
(for all heads of households, under 65)

Non-manual, non-routine		Others	
Executives	643	Clerical workers	133
Professionals	375	Military/security	114
Sales agents	283	Operatives	111
White collar supervisors	270	Craftsmen	106
Industrial supervisors	256	Retail sales	95
Educators	224	Service workers	94
Employers	210	Peddlers	89
Technicians	197	Laborers	75
Merchants	140	Domestic workers	65
		Agricultural workers	43

Source: ENIGH-2000
Note: Median for all occupations = 100

TABLE C.2   Earnings of male heads by age and occupational category
(index of median earnings)

Age (years)	Non-manual, non-routine	Others
25–35	100	100
35–44	127	100
45–54	145	94
55+	91	76

Source: ENIGH-2000
Note: Index for youngest workers in each occupational category = 100

Wilkins 1981; Granato and Mostkoff 1990; Lorey and Linares 1993), which draws on a tradition reaching back to Iturriaga's classic comparison of class structure in 1895 and 1940 (Iturriaga 1951; also Cline 1961, 1967). The SALA estimates of the size of the privileged classes are much larger than my own. In the most recent of the SALA articles, Lorey and Linares (1993) place 45 percent of the population in the privileged classes in 1990 (38 percent as middle class and 7 percent as upper class). This estimate seems problematic for a country in which, ten years later, 60 percent of families still did not have telephones and

65 percent did not have automobiles—two essentials of middle-class life (ENIGH-2000). My own comparable estimate of the middle class (which includes an upper class of statistically trivial size) for 1989 is 16.1 percent (ENIGH-1989).

What accounts for this enormous difference? The SALA estimates are made with aggregate occupation and income statistics from the decennial census. Separate estimates of the class structure are produced for occupation and income and then the two are averaged to produce a composite estimate. (For example, if 20 percent of the population have middle-class occupations and 40 percent have middle-class incomes, then 30 percent may be considered middle class.) For the occupation estimate, low-level office and sales workers are counted as middle class. The income estimate is based on a hierarchy of absolute income levels representing distinct living standards; these were originally conceived in the 1950s and have only been adjusted for inflation to produce the recent estimates. (The implicit, though perhaps unintended, assumption is that a middle-class or lower-class standard of living was the same in 2000 as it had been in 1950.) For the estimates in this book, (1) lower-white-collar workers are not counted as middle class, (2) a relative income threshold is used to take account of rising living standards, and (3) occupation and income distinctions are simultaneously applied to household-level data to determine class status, household by household. These three elements of the current methodology contribute to smaller estimates of the middle class.

NOTES

Chapter 1

1. To preserve confidentiality, aliases are used throughout this work. Occasionally personal details have been blurred for the same purpose.

2. For more on Cuernavaca and the Cuernavaca sample, see appendix B.

3. The surveys used are described in the preface and appendix A.

4. These Cuernavaca homes are probably larger than those of families at equivalent levels in the largest metropolitan areas, especially Mexico City.

5. See, for examples, the "Communist Manifesto," the "Eighteenth Brumaire," and *Theories of Surplus Value*, available in multiple editions.

6. Marx called those who own small enterprises that employ little or no non-family labor "petty bourgeois." The label does not clarify their relations with other classes or other middle sector groups.

7. Weber wrote about class and status (prestige) as alternative dimensions of stratification. Here the discussion is limited to class.

8. See Iturriaga 1951; Cline 1961 and 1962; Stern and Kahl 1968; Lorey and Linares 1993.

9. Another example: in some data sets, white collar supervisors are lumped in the same category as the low-level office workers.

10. This figure refers to households defined and national household data analyzed as described later in this chapter.

11. This figure was derived from the alternative exchange rates published by the Organisation for Economic Co-operation and Development. Called "purchasing power parities," they are designed to more accurately reflect the relative worth of national currencies (OECD 2005).

12. Long experience with this standard survey question has shown that the distribution of responses is very sensitive to the answer categories offered (Gilbert 2003: 212–13). The categories employed here, which were translated from English, seem problematic in the Mexican context. The addition of the commonly used *clase popular* (popular class) to the list might, for example, have produced different results.

13. For more detailed information on measuring the middle class with ENIGH data see appendix C.

14. This estimate is smaller than some, in particular, the frequently cited series of estimates produced for the *Statistical Abstract of Latin America* (SALA), which are

based on more liberal criteria and less detailed information. See appendix C for differences with the SALA estimates.

15. ENIGH documentation (INEGI-2001c) defines the head of household as the individual recognized as such by other members of the household. Only rarely is the recorded head a married woman. On the other hand, if the head were less subjectively defined as the principal income earner, the data indicate that the distribution of heads by gender and marital status would change little. Of course, the proportion of female-headed households would be larger if those with heads over 64 were not excluded from the analysis.

16. The figure for metropolitan areas is from ENIGH-1996 data and is probably an underestimate. ENIGH-2000 did not differentiate among cities over 100,000.

17. See Tarrés 1987: 146; Icazuriaga M. 1994: 449; Tarrés 1999: 428; Gilbert and Varley 1991: 32–38.

18. Of course, there is no way of knowing the extent to which interviewers' estimations of race were influenced by the class markers exhibited by respondents or by their own class and racial identities.

Chapter 2

1. The term is most commonly applied to the period 1946 to 1970, but even in the sometimes problematic 1970s, GDP growth exceeded 6 percent (Mattar et al. 2003: 127).

2. By one estimate, 83 percent of middle-class workers in 1956 were employed in the tertiary sector (Kahl 1968: 19). According to ENIGH data, 75 percent of the heads of middle-class households held tertiary sector jobs in 2000 (ENIGH-2000).

3. See appendix A for information on this survey, which is further analyzed in chapter 5.

4. For a more detailed discussion of the SALA series see appendix C.

5. Oliveira and Roberts include employers, managers, professionals, and technicians in their "higher non-manual strata." Semi-professionals such as teachers are apparently included among professionals. Many of the employers included would have been medium farmers. The authors did not consider income.

6. Mobility in the study refers to movement among six occupational categories, three manual and three non-manual.

7. Readers of Gabriel García Márquez's *One Hundred Years of Solitude* will recall that the child bride Remedios had a similar problem, though not rooted in paternal abuse. For his part, García Márquez claims to invent nothing.

Chapter 3

1. See the analysis in chapter 8 for further details.

2. Mexicans typically refer to the crisis as the "Error of December," a phrase that casts primary responsibility on the Zedillo administration, which assumed power that month. The choice is ironic, since it appears that most Mexicans blame the outgoing Salinas administration.

3. Based on ENIGH household data. See the analysis in chapter 8 for further details.

4. This family was the only one to actually lose its home. Two others, more willing

to endure an extended legal struggle, were still living in houses claimed by the bank. One merchant lost a valuable commercial lot.

5. The domestic cycle describes the successive stages of child bearing, maturation, and dispersion of offspring resulting from a domestic union. See discussion in Gonzalez de la Rocha 1994: 20–28. For the distribution of the Cuernavaca families across the domestic cycle, see appendix B, table B.2c.

Chapter 4

1. Bourdieu's conception of cultural capital emphasizes the informal knowledge absorbed by children growing up in privileged homes, a topic beyond the scope of this research.

2. See references to the relevant literature in the bibliographic notes.

3. On the domestic cycle, see Gonzalez de la Rocha 1994: 20–28. For the distribution of the Cuernavaca families across the domestic cycle, see appendix B, table B.2c.

4. The 2000 ENIGH data also reveal that among young adults 18 to 21, 70 percent of middle-class and 24 percent of popular-class family members are in school at some level.

Chapter 5

1. The class composition of the movement reflected its origins on elite campuses. For example, in the 1960s, only 16 percent of UNAM students were children of workers or peasants. Ninety-one percent were drawn from the richest 15 percent of the population (Zermeño 1978: 48).

2. The government may have also have been troubled by signs of youth rebellion at provincial universities (Lee 2001).

Chapter 6

1. López Portillo had earlier contributed to Echeverría's fatal policies as his finance minister.

2. The figures for lower occupational categories were similar. All refer to percentages of respondents who expressed a preference, excluding the 25 to 30 percent who did not.

3. See Almond and Verba 1963; Fagen and Tuohy 1972; Moreno 2003; Booth and Seligson 1984; Craig and Cornelius 1989.

4. Because of dissimilarities in the samples (the civic culture study was limited to the urban population), the wording of questions, and the socioeconomic categories used to define class, it is impossible to say whether class differences have widened or narrowed. However, gross differences between 1959 and 2000 polls suggest the following changes over time: (1) middle-class respondents are now significantly more likely to reject the antidemocratic "strong man" proposition than they were in the past, (2) both middle-class and other respondents are substantially less likely to subscribe to the "people take advantage of you" proposition that suggests a low level of social trust (see the following footnote on trust), and (3) respondents at both class levels are more likely to belong to voluntary organizations. These statements refer to comparisons with items e, i, and j in table 6.1.

5. In 1959, about 95 percent of respondents at both class levels agreed that "people take advantage of you if you don't watch out" (Civic Culture-1959). By 2000 agreement with a similar item had dropped into the 60s (see table 6.1). Responses to another item suggesting that "most people can be trusted" seem to have changed much less dramatically in the opposite direction—that is, toward less trust. But see the preceding footnote regarding measurement of change. Class differences are insignificantly small on all these trust items. For an empirical test casting doubt on the presumed relationship between democratization and trust, see McClintock and Lebovic 2006.

6. Among respondents in the middle-class occupational, income, and educational categories, support for change ranged from 56 to 66 percent.

7. See the discussion at the beginning of chapter 3 and table 8.2 in chapter 8. The available data suggest that relative to popular-class incomes, middle-class incomes rise faster in boom periods and fall faster in periods of economic crisis.

Chapter 7

1. The tiny PAN/PRI percentage differences among popular voters in 2000 and among middle-class voters in 1994 are not statistically significant.

2. The circumscribed character of the socioeconomic information on households collected for the panel study meant that the class position (as understood here) of most respondents could not be determined. The analysis was limited to a subsample of 141 middle-class and 592 popular-class respondents drawn from late waves of the panel study. Among these respondents, middle-class voters favored the PAN over the PRI, 53 to 26 percent, and popular-class voters gave PAN 41 percent and PRI 40 percent, a statistical tie.

3. Employment sector is based on an item asking whether the respondent worked in the public sector or the private sector or was self-employed (*por cuenta propia*). The latter category includes both employers and non-employers. Middle-class respondents classified as por cuenta propia would include small-business owners and independent professionals. Among popular-class respondents in this category there is probably a significant proportion of street peddlers.

Chapter 8

1. Another foreign writer picked up similar notions from the Mexicans he interviewed. The index to Earl Shorris's book, *The Life and Times of Mexico* (2004) contains numerous page references under the heading "middle class, the decline of."

2. Only 12 percent of popular-class families with middle-class incomes (over 150 percent of the household median) had computers in 2000.

3. Senior high school level institutions, including preparatory normal schools, and other specialized schools.

4. The percentage of primary school students in private schools rose from 4.8 in 1984 to 7.6 percent in 2000, a period when the primary school attendance rate was rising generally. Note that these figures from the Secretaría de Educación Pública do not take into account school age children who were not in school.

5. Because the household survey did not ask about current school enrollment in

1984, the figures for that year were estimated with national matriculation statistics and ENIGH data.

Epilogue

1. I am grateful to Roy Campos and Luis Fernando Asiain of Consulta Mitofsky for providing the exit poll data on which table E.1 is based. Because the Mitofsky poll did not collect occupational data, I used income and education to identify middle-class voters. When this income-education standard was applied to the *LA Times/ Reforma* data analyzed in chapter 7, it produced estimates within 2 percent of those based on income and occupation.

Appendix B

1. According to an official of ANTAD, the national association of chain stores, lower-class Mexicans are less likely than middle-class Mexicans to patronize the big chains. The companies see their market as largely middle class.

2. Families of origin were considered middle class based on non-routine white collar occupation, comfortable lifestyle, or respondents' private school attendance. Information about grandparents was generally less detailed, but approximately 40 percent of respondents' paternal grandparents appear to be middle class.

BIBLIOGRAPHIC NOTES

Chapter 1

There is ample material on Cuernavaca in Moctezuma Navarro and Tapia Uribe, *Morelos: El Estado* (1993). For the city's demographic trends, see Dirección General de Estadística 1962: 68; INEGI 2001a; and Garza 2003. Also consulted were Pike and Butler 1997: 40–44; Dillon 1999; *Enciclopedia de México* 1988: 5618; Womack 1968; and Lomnitz-Adler 1992.

Edgell's *Class* (1993) and Vidich, ed., *The New Middle Class* (1995), provide lucid introductions to the problems of defining the middle class. Also useful were Abercrombie and Urry 1983 and Wacquant 1991. For Marx's own thinking, see especially the "Communist Manifesto" and the "Eighteenth Brumaire," both available in numerous editions of his works. Weber's ideas are most systematically presented in Weber 1958: 180–95. For neo-Marxist formulations, see Wright 1976; Wright 1985; and Carchedi 1977. For neo-Weberian approaches, see Goldthorpe 1982; Giddens 1973; Lockwood 1989; and Mills 1956.

Previous work on the Mexican middle class includes Loaeza, *Clases Medias y Política en México* (1988); Loaeza and Stern, eds., *Las clases medias en la coyuntura actual* (1990); Whetten 1970; and López Cámara 1971 and 1988. For alternative estimates of the size of the middle class, see Stern and Kahl 1968; Lorey and Linares 1993; and the sources these works cite. Also see the discussion in appendix C.

Chapter 2

Important sources for Mexico in the 1940s and its transformation during the Growth Decades include Aguilar Camín and Meyer, *In the Shadow of the Mexican Revolution* (1993); Niblo, *Mexico in the 1940s* (1999); and Cline, *Mexico: Revolution to Evolution* (1962). Also useful were Moreno 2003; Hansen 1971; Sherman 2000; Stern and Kahl 1968; and Bethell 1998. Garza, *La Urbanización de México en el siglo xx* (2003), is the best recent account of urbanization and demographic trends. Studies of social mobility in the Growth Era include Reyna 1963; Contreras Suarez 1978; and Zenteno 2002. Lorey 1993 treats the role of higher education.

Chapter 3

On the collapse of the Mexican miracle and introduction of neoliberal policies, see especially Lustig, *Mexico: The Remaking of an Economy* (1998). Also see Ros and Lustig 2003; Pastor and Wise 2003; and Nadal 2003.

Chapter 4

A rich social science literature has explored the survival strategies of Mexican households in the face of economic adversity, though there is relatively little on middle-class households. Major works include González de la Rocha, *The Resources of Poverty* (1994); Selby et al., *The Mexican Urban Household* (1990); and Lomnitz, *Networks and Marginality* (1977). Also useful were Benería 1992; González de la Rocha 1995; Gonzalez de la Rocha and Lapatí 1991; and Murphy and Stepick 1991.

Chapters 5 and 6

These chapters draw on several general accounts of the political history of modern Mexico, including Krauze, *Mexico, Biography of Power* (1998); Aguilar Camín and Meyer 1993; Bethell 1991; Cline 1962; Kandell 1988; and Knight 1991. For recent decades, three books by foreign journalists were helpful: Riding, *Distant Neighbors* (1984); Oppenheimer, *Bordering on Chaos* (1996); and Preston and Dillon, *Opening Mexico* (2004). Loaeza traces the political history of the middle class from the 1920s to the early 1960s in *Clases Medias y Política en México* (1988).

The literature of the 1910 revolution is vast. A good place to start is Knight 1990. My treatment of "the Revolution" as political myth and Mexican political culture more generally draws on Segovia 1975; Kahl 1968; Almond and Verba 1963; Craig and Cornelius 1989; O'Malley 1986; and Gilbert 1997 and 2002.

Most of the general accounts of recent political history mentioned earlier provide fairly detailed chronologies of the 1968 student movement and the Tlatelolco massacre. See Krauze 1998: 694–731; Preston and Dillon 2004: 63–93; and Kandell 1988: 519–527. Poniatowska's *La noche de Tlatelolco* (1971; in English, 1975) is worth attention both as oral history and as a powerful political document that influenced Mexican popular perceptions of the event. Other important interpretations include Aguayo 1998 and Zermeño 1978. Zolov 1999 places the 1968 movement in the context of the international youth culture of the late 1960s. Jorge Fons's influential feature film *Rojo Amanecer* (1989, available on DVD) emphasizes the intergenerational tensions that interest Zolov. On the 1985 earthquake, see Poniatowska 1995, as well as Preston and Dillon 2004, who also present a first-rate account of the 1988 election.

Chapter 7

For the 2000 elections, I've consulted Preston and Dillon 2004, who covered the campaign for the *New York Times*; Moreno 2003; and the essays in Dominguez and Lawson 2004. Dominguez and McCann 1998 examined the 1988 and 1994 elections. Craig and Cornelius 1989, as well as Moreno 2003, stress the importance of social class in political opinion. For an analysis skeptical of the independence significance of social class, see Dominguez and McCann 1998; Lawsen and Klesner 2004, as well as Klesner 2004, seem implicitly to share this view.

Chapter 8

For the economics of the 1990s, I have drawn on the same sources listed above for chapter 3 and the World Bank Web site.

BIBLIOGRAPHY

Survey data sources are cited as indicated in appendix A. In addition to the published sources listed below, the following Web sites were consulted: Instituto Nacional de Estadística, Geografía e Informática, www.inegi.gob.mx; Organization for Economic Co-operation and Development, www.oecd.org; Secretaría de Educación Pública, www.sep.gob.mx; World Bank, www.worldbank.org.

Abercrombie, Nicholas, and John Urry. 1983. *Capital, Labour and the Middle Classes.* Boston: George Allen & Unwin.

Adams, David. 1995. "Coping with Less: Peso Devaluation Hits Mexico's Middle Class Where It Hurts." *Rocky Mountain News*, January 23.

Aguilar Camin, Hector, and Lorenzo Meyer. 1993. *In the Shadow of the Mexican Revolution: Contemporary Mexican History, 1910–1989.* Austin: University of Texas Press.

Aguayo Quezada, Sergio. 1998. *1968: Los archivos de la violencia.* Mexico: Grijalbo and Reforma.

Aguayo Quezada, Sergio. 2000. *Almanaque México: Compendio Exhaustivo de México.* Mexico City: Grupo Editorial Grijalbo.

Almond, Gabriel A., and Sidney Verba. 1963. *The Civic Culture: Political Attitudes and Democracy in Five Nations.* Princeton, N.J.: Princeton University Press.

Almond, Gabriel A., and Sidney Verba, eds. 1989. *The Civic Culture Revisited.* Newbury Park, Calif.: Sage Publications.

ANTAD (Associación Nacional de Tiendas de Autoservicio y Departmentales). 1999. *Directorio 1999.* Mexico City: ANTAD.

Basáñez, Miguel. 1999. *El Pulso de los Sexenios: 20 años de crisis en México.* Mexico City: Siglo vientiuno editores.

Beltrán, Ulises et al. 1996. *Los Mexicanos de los Noventa.* Mexico City: Instituto de Investigaciones Sociales, UNAM.

Benería, Lourdes. 1992. "The Mexican Debt Crisis: Restructuring the Economy and the Household." In *Unequal Burden, Economic Crises, Persistent Poverty and Women's Work,* ed. Lourdes Benería and Shelley Feldman. Boulder, Colo.: Westview Press.

Bethell, Leslie, ed. 1991. *Mexico Since Independence.* Cambridge: Cambridge University Press.

——. 1998. *Latin America: Economy and Society Since 1930.* Cambridge: Cambridge University Press.

Boltvinik, Julio. 1994. *Pobreza y Estratificación social en México.* Instituto Nacional de Estadística Geografía e Informática.

Booth, John, and Mitchell Seligson. 1984. "The Political Culture of Authoritarianism in Mexico." *Latin American Research Review* 19: 106–24.

Bourdieu, Pierre. 1986. "The Forms of Capital." In *Handbook of Theory and Research for the Sociology of Education,* ed. John G. Richardson. New York: Greenwood Press.

Burris, Val. 1995. "The Discovery of the New Middle Classes." In *The New Middle Class,* ed. Vidich.

Carchedi, Guglielmo. 1977. *On the Economic Identification of Social Classes.* London: Routledge and Kegan Paul.

Cline, Howard F. 1961. *The United States and Mexico.* Cambridge, Mass.: Harvard University Press.

——. 1962. *Mexico: Revolution to Evolution.* New York: Oxford University Press.

——. 1967. *The United States and Mexico.* Rev. ed. Cambridge, Mass.: Harvard University Press.

Contreras Suárez, Enrique. 1978. *Estratificación Social en la Cuidad de Mexico.* Mexico City: UNAM.

Cortés, Fernando. 2000. *La Distribución del ingreso en México en épocas de estabilización y reforma económica.* Mexico City: Miguel Angel Porrua.

Craig, Ann L., and Wayne A. Cornelius. 1989. "Political Culture in Mexico: Continuities and Revisionist Interpretations." In *The Civic Culture Revisited,* ed. Almond and Verba.

Dettmer, Jorge, and Aurora Loyo. 1997. "El Debate sobre la educación básica." In *El Debate Nacional,* ed. Valencia and Barba.

Dillon, Sam. 1999. "Mexico City Spawns Suburbs, Changing the Face of Countryside." *New York Times,* December 18.

Domínguez, Jorge I., and Chappell Lawson, eds. 2004. *Mexico's Pivotal Democratic Election: Candidates, Voters, and the Presidential Campaign of 2000.* Stanford, Calif.: Stanford University Press.

Domínguez, Jorge I., and James McCann. 1998. *Democratizing Mexico: Public Opinion and Electoral Choices.* Baltimore: Johns Hopkins University Press.

Dussel Peters, Enrique. 2000. *Polarizing Mexico: The Impact of Liberalization Strategy.* Boulder, Colo.: Lynne Rienner.

Edgell, Stephen. 1993. *Class.* New York: Routledge.

Enciclopedia de México. 1988. Mexico City: Editora de Enciclopedia de México.

Fagen, Richard R., and William S. Tuohy, eds. 1972. *Politics and Privilege in a Mexican City.* Stanford, Calif.: Stanford University Press.

Ffrench-Davis, Ricardo. 1998. "The Latin American Economies, 1950–1990." In *Latin America,* ed. Bethell.

Fuentes Molinar, Olac. 1991. "Educación Pública y Sociedad." In *México, Hoy,* ed. Pablo González Casanova and Enrique Florescano. Mexico City: Siglo Veintiuno.

Garza, Gustavo. 2003. *La urbanización de México en el siglo xx.* Mexico City: Colegio de México.

Giddens, Anthony. 1973. *The Class Structure of Advanced Societies.* New York: Harper and Row.

Gilbert, Alan, and Ann Varley 1991. *Landlord and Tenant: Housing the Poor in Urban Mexico.* New York: Routledge.

Gilbert, Dennis. 1997. "Rewriting History: Salinas, Zedillo, and the 1992 Textbook Controversy." *Mexican Studies/Estudios Mexicanos* 13: 271–98.

——. 2002. "Emiliano Zapata: Textbook Hero." *Mexican Studies/Estudios Mexicanos* 19: 127–60.

——. 2003. *The American Class Structure in an Age of Growing Inequality.* 6th ed. Belmont, Calif.: Wadsworth.

——. 2005a. "Magicians: The Response of Middle-Class Mexican Households to Economic Crisis." *Journal of Latin American Anthropology* 10: 126–50.

——. 2005b. "La clase media mexicana y la crisis economica de mediados de los años noventa." *Estudios Sociológicos* 68: 465–83.

Goldthorpe, John. 1982. "Service Class." In *Social Class and the Division of Labour,* ed. Anthony Giddens and Gavin Mackenzie. Cambridge: Cambridge University Press.

González Casanova, Pablo. 1965. *La Democracia en México.* Mexico City: Ediciones Era.

——. 1968. "Dynamics of the Class Structure." In *Comparative Perspectives on Stratification,* ed. Kahl.

González de la Rocha, Mercedes. 1994. *The Resources of Poverty: Women and Survival in a Mexican City.* Oxford: Basil Blackwell.

——. 1995. "Social Restructuring in Two Mexican Cities: An Analysis of Domestic Groups in Guadalajara and Monterrey." *European Journal of Development Research* 7: 389–406.

——. 2001. "From the Resources of Poverty to the Poverty of Resources? The Erosion of a Survival Model." *Latin American Perspectives* 28: 72–100.

González de la Rocha, Mercedes, and Agustin Escobar Latapí, eds. 1991. *Social Responses to Mexico's Economic Crisis of the 1980s.* San Diego: University of San Diego, Center for U.S.–Mexican Studies.

Granato, Stephanie, and Aida Mostkoff. 1990. "The Class Structure of Mexico, 1895–1980." In *Society and Economy in Mexico: Statistical Abstract of Latin America,* ed. James Wilkie. Supplement 10. Los Angeles: UCLA Latin American Center Publications.

Guitiérrez Garza, Esthela, Enrique Valencia, and Carlos Barba. 1997. *El Debate Nacional: 5. la Política Social.* Mexico City: Universidad de Guadalajara.

Hansen, Roger D. 1971. *The Politics of Mexican Development.* Baltimore: Johns Hopkins University Press.

Hewitt de Alcántara, Cynthia. 1977. *Ensayo sobre la satisfacción de necesidades básicas del pueblo Mexicano entre 1940 y 1970.* Mexico City: El Colegio de México.

Houston Chronicle (Jenalia Moreno) 2002. "Mexico's Struggling Middle Class." September 1.

Icazuriaga Montes, Carmen. 1994. "Desaggo urbana y forma de vida de la clase media en la ciudad de Querétaro." *Estudios Demográficos y Urbanos.* 9: 439–57.

INEGI (Instituto Nacional de Estadística, Geografía e Informática). 1997. *Cuaderno Estadístico Municipal: Cuernavaca, Estado de Morelos.*

——. 2000. *Encuesta Nacional de Empleo Urbano.* Online at www.inegi.gob.mx.

——. 2001a. *Estadísticas sociodemográficas: Las Ciudades con Más Población 1990 y 1995.* Online at www.inegi.gob.mx.

——. 2001b. Indicatores Sociodemográficos (1930–2000).

——. 2001c. ENIGH 2000. *Encuesta Nacional de Ingresos y Gastos de los Hogares.*

Iturriaga, José. 1951. *La Estructura Social y Cultural de México*. Mexico City: Fundo de Cultura Económica.

Johnson, John J. 1967. *Political Change in Latin America: The Emergence of the Middle Sectors*. Stanford, Calif.: Stanford University Press.

Kahl, Joseph, ed. 1968. *Comparative Perspectives on Stratification: Mexico, Great Britain, Japan*. Boston: Little, Brown and Co.

Kandell, Jonathan. 1988. *La Capital: The Biography of Mexico City*. New York: Henry Holt.

Klesner, Joseph. 2004. "The Structure of the Mexican Electorate: Social, Attitudinal and Partisan Bases of Vicente Fox's Victory." In *Mexico's Pivotal Democratic Election*, ed. Domínguez and Lawson.

Knight, Alan. 1990. *The Mexican Revolution*. 2 vols. Lincoln: University of Nebraska Press.

———. 1991. "The Rise and Fall of Cardenismo, c. 1930–1946." In *Mexico Since Independence*, ed. Bethell.

Kohn, Melvin. 1969. *Class and Conformity: A Study in Values*. Homewood, Ill.: Dorsey Press.

Kohn, Melvin, and Carmi Schooler. 1983. *Work and Personality: An Inquiry into the Impact of Social Stratification*. Norwood, N.J.: ABLEX.

Krauze, Enrique. 1998. *Mexico, Biography of Power: A History of Modern Mexico 1810–1996*. New York: HarperCollins.

Lawson, Chappell, and Joseph Klesner. 2004. "Political Reform, Electoral Participation, and the Campaign of 2000." In *Mexico's Pivotal Democratic Election*, ed. Domínguez and Lawson.

Lee, Erik. 2001. *Tambien pasó aquí: Student Movements in Sonora and Sinaloa 1966–1974*. Masters thesis, University of California, San Diego.

Lewis, Oscar. 1951. *Life in a Mexican Village: Tepotzlán Revisited*. Urbana: University of Illinois Press.

Loaeza, Soledad. 1988. *Clases Medias y Política en México: La Querella Escolar, 1959–63*. Mexico City: Colegio de México.

———. 1998. "El estudio de las clases medias mexicanas después de 1940." *Estudios Políticos* 3, no. 2 (April–June): 52–62.

Loaeza, Soledad, and Claudio Stern, eds. 1990. *Las clases medias en la coyuntura actual*. Mexico City: Colegio de México.

Lockwood, David. 1989. *The Black-coated Worker: A Study in Class Consciousness*. 2d ed. Oxford: Oxford University Press.

Lomnitz, Larissa. 1977. *Networks and Marginality: Life in a Mexican Shantytown*. New York: Academic Press.

Lomnitz-Adler, Claudio. 1992. *Exits from the Labyrinth: Culture and Ideology in the Mexican National Space*. Berkeley: University of California Press.

López Cámara, Francisco. 1971. *El Desafío de la Clase Media*. Mexico City: Editorial Joaquin Mortiz.

López Cámara, Francisco, ed. 1988. *La Clase Media en la Era del Populismo*. Mexico City: Miguel Angel Porrúa.

López Portillo, José. 1988. "Un reto de la Democracia en México: La Incorporación Institucional de las Clases Medias." Anexo II. In *La Clase Media en la Era del Populismo*, ed. López Cámara.

Lorey, David. 1993. *The University System and Economic Development in Mexico Since 1929*. Stanford, Calif.: Stanford University Press.

Lorey, David, and Aida Moskoff Linares. 1993. "Mexico's Lost Decade, 1980–90: Evidence on Class Structure and Professional Employment from the 1990 Census." In *Statistical Abstract of Latin America*, ed. James Wilkie. Vol. 30, part 2. Los Angeles: UCLA Latin American Center.

Lustig, Nora. 1998. *Mexico: The Remaking of an Economy*. Washington, D.C.: Brookings Institution Press.

Marum Espinosa, Elia. 1997. "Formación y capacitación de recursos humanos de alto nivel para la competitividad en México." In *El Debate Nacional*, ed. Valencia and Barba.

Máttar, Jorge, et al. 2003. "Foreign Investment in Mexico after Economic Reform." In *Confronting Development*, ed. Middlebrook and Zapeda.

Marx, Karl. 1963–1972. *Theories of Surplus Value*. 3 vols. London: Lawrence & Wishart.

McClintock, Cynthia, and James Lebovic. 2006. "Correlates of Levels of Democracy in Latin American during the 1990s." *Latin American Politics and Society* 48: 29–59.

Mendieta Nuñez, Lucio. 1955. "La Clase Media en México." *Revista mexicana de sociología*. 17: 517–31.

Merrick, Thomas. 1998. "The Population of Latin America, 1930–1990." In *Latin America*, ed. Bethell.

Meyer, Michael C., and William H. Beezley, eds. 2000. *The Oxford History of Mexico*. New York: Oxford University Press.

Middlebrook, Kevin, and Eduardo Zepeda, eds. 2003. *Confronting Development: Assessing Mexico's Economic and Social Development*. Stanford, Calif.: Stanford University Press.

Mills, C. Wright. 1956. *White Collar: The American Middle Classes*. New York: Oxford University Press.

Moctezuma Nevarro, David, and Medardo Tapia Uribe. 1993. *Morelos: El Estado*. Cuernavaca: Government of Morelos.

Moreno, Alejandro. 2003. *El Votante Mexicano: Democracia, actitudes políticas y conducta electoral*. Mexico City: Fondo de Cultura Económica.

Moreno, Julio. 2003. *Yankee Don't Go Home: American Business Culture and the Shaping of Modern Mexico, 1920–1950*. Chapel Hill, N.C.: University of North Carolina Press.

Motor Vehicle Facts and Figures, 1986–2002. Detroit: American Automobile Manufacturers Association (1986–98). Southfield, Mich.: Ward's Communications (2000–2002).

Murphy, Arthur, and Alex Stepick. 1991. *Social Inequality in Oaxaca: A History of Resistance and Change*. Philadelphia: Temple University Press.

Nadal, Alejandro. 2003. "Macroeconomic Challenges for Mexico's Development Strategy." In *Confronting Development*, ed. Middlebrook and Zepeda.

New York Times (Ginger Thompson). 2002. "Free-Market Upheaval Grinds Mexico's Middle Class." September 4.

Niblo, Stephen R. 1999. *Mexico in the 1940s: Modernity, Politics, and Corruption*. Wilmington, Del.: SR Books.

Oliveira, Orlandina, and Bryan Roberts. 1998. "Urban Social Structures in Latin America, 1939–1990." In *Latin America*, ed. Bethell.

O'Malley, Ilene. 1986. *The Myth of the Revolution: Hero Cults and the Institutionaliza-tion of the Mexican State, 1920–1940*. New York: Greenwood Press.

Ongay, Mario. 1979. "La Familia de las Clases Medias en México." *Revista Mexicana de Ciencias Políticas y Sociales* 25–26: 5–81.

Oppenheimer, Andres. 1996. *Bordering on Chaos*. Boston: Little, Brown and Company.

Organization for Economic Co-operation and Development (OECD). 2005. "Purchasing Power Parities." *Main Economic Indicators*, January. Online at www.oecd.org/std/ppp.

Othón de Mendizábal, M., et al. 1970. *Ensayos Sobre las Clases Sociales en México*. 2nd ed. Mexico City: Nuestro Tiempo.

Pardinas, Juan. 2004. "Fighting Poverty in Mexico: Policy Challenges." In *Mexico Under Fox*, ed. Luis Rubio and Susan Kaufman Purcell. Boulder, Colo.: Lynn Rienner.

Parker, David. 1998. *The Idea of the Middle Class: White Collar Workers and Peruvian Society*. University Park: Pennsylvania State University Press.

Pastor, Manuel, and Carol Wise. 2003. "A Long View of Mexico's Political Economy: What's Changed? What Are the Challenges?" In *Mexico's Politics and Society in Transition*, ed. Joseph Tulchin and Andrew Selee. Boulder, Colo.: Lynne Rienner.

Prawda, Juan. 1987. *Logros, Inequidades y Retos del Futuro del Sistema Educativo Mexicano*. 4to Edición. Mexico City: Colección Pedagógica Grijalbo.

Pike, James, and Edgar Butler. 1997. *Mexico Megacity*. Boulder, Colo.: Westview Press.

Poniatowska, Elena. 1971. *La noche de Tlatelolco: Testimonios de historia oral*. Mexico City: Ediciones Era.

——. 1975. *Massacre in Mexico*. New York: Viking.

——. 1995. *Nothing, Nobody: The Voices of the Mexico City Earthquake*. Philadelphia: Temple University Press.

Preston, Julia, and Samuel Dillon. 2004. *Opening Mexico: The Making of a Democracy*. New York: Farrar, Straus and Giroux.

Redfield, Robert. 1930. *Tepotzlán: A Mexican Village*. Chicago: University of Chicago Press.

Reyes Heroles, Jesús. 1988. "Hacia la organización política de las clases medias Mexicanas." Anexo I. In *La Clase Media en la Era del Populismo*, ed. Francisco López Cámara.

Reyna, José Luis. 1968. "Some Patterns of Occupational Mobility: The Mexican Case." *Social Research, the International Scene: Current Trends in the Social Sciences* 35: 540–64.

Riding, Alan. 1985. *Distant Neighbors: A Portrait of the Mexicans*. New York: Alfred A. Knopf.

Ros, Jaime, and Nora Claudia Lustig. 2003. "Economic Liberalization and Income Distribution in Mexico: Losers and Winners in a Time of Global Restructuring." In *Struggles for Social Rights in Latin America*, ed. Susan Eva Eckstein and Timothy Wickham-Crowley. New York: Routledge.

Rubalcava, Rosa Maria. 1999. "El ingreso de los hogares en México: Una visión de dos décadas." In *La situación demográfica de México, 1999*. Mexico City: Consejo Nacional de Población.

Segovia, Rafael. 1975. *La Politización del Niño Mexicano*. Mexico City: El Colegio de México.

Selby, Henry, et al. 1990. *The Mexican Urban Household: Organizing for Self-Defense*. Austin: University of Texas Press.

Sherman, John. 2000. "The Mexican 'Miracle' and Its Collapse." In *The Oxford History of Mexico*, ed. Meyer and Beezley.

Shorris, Earl. 2004. *The Life and Times of Mexico*. New York: Norton.

Stern, Claudio. 1990. "Notas para la delimitación de las clases medianas en México." In Loaeza and Stern, eds.

Stern, Claudio, and Joseph Kahl. 1968. "Stratification Since the Revolution." In *Comparative Perspectives on Stratification*, ed. Kahl.

Tarrés, María Luisa. 1987 "Crisis and Political Opposition Among the Mexican Middle Classes." *International Sociology* 2: 131–50.

———. 1999. "Vida en Familia: Prácticas privadas y discursos públicos en las clases medias de Ciudad Satélite." *Estudios Sociológicos* 17, no. 50: 419–37.

Thorp, Rosemary. 1998. "The Latin American Economies, 1930–1950." In *Latin America*, ed. Bethell.

U.S. Department of Labor. 2000. *Report on the Youth Labor Force*. Washington, D.C.: U.S. Department of Labor.

Valencia, Enrique, and Carlos Barba, eds. 1997. *El Debate Nacional: 5. La Política Social*. Mexico City: Editorial Diana.

Vidich, Arthur. 1995. *The New Middle Class: Life-Styles, Status Claims, and Political Orientations*. New York: New York University Press.

Wacquant, Loic, J. D. 1991. "Making Class: The Middle Class(es) in Social Theory and Social Structure." In *Bringing Class Back In: Contemporary and Historical Perspectives*, ed. Scott G. McNall et al. Boulder, Colo.: Westview Press.

Weber, Max. 1958. *From Max Weber: Essays in Sociology*. New York: Oxford University Press.

Whetten, Nathan. 1970. "El Surgimiento de una Clase Media en México." In *Ensayos sobre las Clases Sociales en México*, ed. Miguel Othón de Mendizábal. Mexico City: Editorial Nuestro Tiempo.

Wilkie, James, and Paul Wilkins. 1981. "Quantifying the Class Structure of Mexico, 1895–1970." In *Statistical Abstract of Latin America* 21: 577–90, ed. James Wilkie. Los Angeles: Latin American Center Publications, UCLA.

Willis, Katie. 2000. "No es fácil, pero es posible: The Maintenance of Middle-Class Women-Headed Households in Mexico." *European Review of Latin American and Caribbean Studies* 69: 29–45.

Womack, John. 1968. *Zapata and the Mexican Revolution*. New York: Vintage Books.

World Motor Vehicle Data. 1998. Detroit: American Automobile Manufacturers Association.

Wright, Erik. 1976. "Class Boundaries in Advanced Capitalist Societies." *New Left Review* 98: 3–41.

———. 1985. *Classes*. London: Verso.

Zenteno, René. 2002. "Polarización de la movilidad social: Transformaciones, crisis y estructura ocupacional." *Demos: Carta Demográfica Sobre México* 15: 17–18.

Zermeño, Sergio. 1978. *México, una democracia utópica: El movimiento estudiantil del 68*. Mexico City: Siglo Vientiuno.

Zolov, Eric. 1999. *Refried Elvis: The Rise of the Mexican Counterculture*. Berkeley: University of California Press.

INDEX

1968 Student Movement. *See* students, university

Abarca, Cuauhtémoc, 77
Acapulco: vacation in, 39, 40
agrarian reforms, 24, 27, 60
Aguayo, Sergio, 77
Alarcón, Francisco (pseudonym), 31, 42, 44
Alemán, Miguel, 60
Almazán, Juan Andreu, 60, 61
Arce, Lili (pseudonym), 70–71
Arroyo, Miguel (pseudonym), 69–70, 86
austerity programs, 37–38, 74, 75, 78
automobile: ownership of, 5, 6, 16, 17(table), 38, 40, 47, 53, 54, 96, 97(table), 103, 117; production of, 95–96
Avila Camacho, Manuel, 60, 61

banking industry, 28, 43, 49–50
Banquero, Carla (pseudonym), 50
Bernal, Julio (pseudonym), 23, 28, 32–33, 35, 36, 39, 85; and Tlatelolco massacre, 71–72
Blancas, Carmen (pseudonym), 32
Blandón, Fernando (pseudonym), 39–40, 47, 55
Bourdieu, Pierre: on capital, 45–46
budgets: household, 13–14, 54, 55
bus service: to Mexico City, 3–4

Calderón, Felipe: election of, 102–4
Campo Militar #1, 70, 71

capital, 45–46. *See also by type*
capitalism, 10, 60
Cárdenas, Cuauhtémoc, 77
Cárdenas, Lázaro, 60, 66
casa chica, 40, 47
Catholic Church, 59–60, 61, 62, 63
Chiapas: Zapatista movement, in, 78
children: in labor force, 51. *See also* teenagers
Civic Culture Study, 63–64, 81, 105–6
civil society: growth of, 76–77
class consciousness, 10, 11
class structure: analyses of, 115–17. *See also* social class
CNOP. *See* National Confederation of Popular Organizations
Coca-Cola, 23
Colonia Roma: and 1985 earthquake, 75
Colosio, Donaldo: assassination of, 78
commuters, 3–4
computers, 5, 6, 97(table), 98, 103
consumption: reducing, 45, 46–48, 53
Contreras, Oscar (pseudonym), 55
corruption, 66
Cuernavaca, 3, 32; as research site, 108–112
cultural capital, 45, 46, 49, 54, 121n1 (chap. 4)

debt, 20, 37, 75
debt crisis, 37, 38, 39–40
Democracia en México, La (Gonzalez Casanova), 101

Desafío de la Clase Media, El (López Cámara), 73–74
Díaz, Porfirio, 24, 59
Díaz Ordaz, Gustavo, 70, 74
Disneyland: travel to, 39, 40
doctors: national strike of, 62
domestic cycle, 43–44, 121n5

earthquake: 1985, 22, 75–76, 83
Echeverría, Luis, 70, 74
economic capital, 45, 46, 53, 54
economic development, 60, 74–75
economic growth, 20, 24, 25–26, 41, 93–94, 103
economic policy: developmentalist, 25–26, 93–94; neoliberal, 41, 94
economy, 20; consumption and, 46–48; financial crises and, 21–22, 37–38; living standards and, 39–40; politics and, 65–66; recovery of, 55–56; under Salinas, 77–79; and social class, 10, 11
education, 5, 17, 27–28, 32, 34, 36, 54, 55, 80; anti–free-text movement and, 62–63; as cultural capital, 46, 49, 54; during Neoliberal Era, 98–99; private, 48–50, 61, 99–101; public, 23, 24, 33
elections: presidential, 20, 58–59, 64, 74, 77, 78, 80, 82–91, 102–4, 106, 122n1 (chap. 7)
Encuesta Nacional de Ingresos y Gastos de los Hogares (ENIGH), 16, 106, 113–115
engañar (to deceive), 78–79, 100
English language: knowledge of, 31
ENIGH. *See* Encuesta Nacional de Ingresos y Gastos de los Hogares
exit polls, 106
exports, 41

families: in Cuernavaca study, 109–12; dependency on, 51–52, 101; middle class, 4–6, 7–9(figs.); Peso Crisis and, 40–44
Federal Electoral Tribunal, 104
financial crisis, 20, 21–22, 37–38, 40–41,

74–75; impact of, 40–44; recovery from, 55–56
Fox, Vicente, 102; election of, 82, 85–86, 87; support for, 88–91
free-market reform, 38
Free Text Program: opposition to, 62–63

Garcia family (pseudonym), 40, 43, 44
gated communities, 19
General Agreement on Tariffs and Trade (GATT), 38
Gonzalez, Vicente (pseudonym), 55
Gonzalez Casanova, Pablo: *La Democracia en México,* 101
grassroots organizations: and 1985 earthquake, 76
Great Depression, 24
Growth Decades/Era, 25, 26, 27, 60–61, 94; middle class expansion during, 28–29; politics of, 57, 64–66; social mobility during, 29–30
Guadalajara, 62

highway construction, 24
homes, 50; middle class, 7–9(figs.), 119n4; ownership of, 5, 6, 16, 17(table), 43–44, 53
hosting, 50
household, 12, 40; budgets, 13–14; in Cuernavaca, 108–12; ENIGH surveys of, 113–15; peso devaluation and, 41–44; head of, 120n15

identity: as middle class, 14, 15
IMF. *See* International Monetary Fund
income, 5, 13–14, 16, 41, 61, 98; and economy, 21, 38; and social class, 17, 117; sources of, 50–51
income distribution, 25
income shock, 41, 78, 95–96, 100
industrial parks: in Cuernavaca, 3, 108
Instituto Nacional de Estadística, Geografía e Informática (INEGI), 106
International Monetary Fund (IMF), 37–38, 74, 75, 78
irrigation projects, 24

Jalapa, 67
Jalisco, 73

kin, 17; help from, 51–52, 54–55

Labastida, Francisco, 87, 91
labor: militancy of, 60
labor force, 4, 33, 51, 55
Lambert, Ricardo (pseudonym), 39, 43, 44
Lavalle, Ramon (pseudonym), 40
law practices, 42–43, 44
literacy, 32
living standards, 12, 16–17, 21, 53, 55; debt crisis and, 39–40; Neoliberal era, 95–101
López Cámara, Francisco: *El Desafío de la Clase Media*, 73–74
López Obrador, Andrés Manuel: and 2006 election, 102–4
López Portillo, José, 37, 38, 73, 74–75; on crisis of conscience, 57–58; on middle class, 93–94
lost decade, 38
luxuries, 13, 16–17, 100

Madero, Francisco, 59
Madrazo, Roberto, 102
Madrid, Miguel de la, 75, 76
malls, 19
managers, 5, 11, 80
Marín, Roberto (pseudonym), 3, 32, 35
Martínez, Efrain (pseudonym), 43, 44, 50–51, 56
Marx, Karl: on social classes, 6, 10
medical practice, 39, 43, 44
medical school, 33
Meléndez, Gabriela (pseudonym), 63
merchants: peso devaluation, 42, 44, 50
Mexican miracle, 20, 25
Mexico City, 24, 26, 31, 83, 108; commuting to, 3–4; and 1985 earthquake, 22, 75–76; Tlatelolco massacre in, 68–72
Mexico 2000 Panel Study, 106–7
middle class: defining, 6, 10–13, 115–17, 123n2; measuring, 113–15; urban residence of, 18–19
migration, 27, 51

military: and Tlatelolco massacre, 68–70, 71
Miranda family (pseudonym), 43
mistresses, 40, 47
Monterrey, 26, 62
Moreno, Ramiro (pseudonym), 44
Muñoz, Florencio (pseudonym), 23, 31–32, 36
Muñoz, Julio (pseudonym), 31–32, 43

NAFTA. *See* North American Free Trade Agreement
National Action Party. *See* Partido Acción Nacional
National Confederation of Popular Organizations (CNOP), 61
neighborhoods: middle-class, 19, 24
Neoliberal Era, 25, 94; education during, 98–99; living standards during, 95–101
neoliberalism, 21, 37–38, 41
Noche de Tlatelolco, La (Poniatowksa), 72
North American Free Trade Agreement (NAFTA), 38, 78, 79

occupation: and social class, 11, 12–13, 28–29, 113–17, 120n5

PAN. *See* Partido Acción Nacional
Pardo, Javier, 46–47
Partido Acción Nacional (PAN), 22, 60, 62, 64, 79, 80; support for, 73–74, 87–91, 122nn1–2 (chap. 7); in 2000 election, 85–86, 91–92; in 2006 election, 102, 103
Partido de la Revolución Democrática (PRD), 80, 102
Partido Revolucionario Institucional (PRI), 42, 73, 76, 94; defeat of, 22, 82–83; elections, 84, 85, 92, 102; and middle class, 57, 58, 61–62, 66; opposition to, 71, 78–79; support for, 64–65, 72, 79–80, 87–91, 122nn1–2 (chap. 7)
peasants, 59, 60, 80
peso: devaluation of, 41, 75, 78
Peso Crisis, 20, 21, 40, 94; impacts of, 41–44

petroleum industry, 74–75

Picón, Angela (pseudonym), 35, 36, 71

political culture: class differences in, 64–65, 80–82

politics, 57, 79; attitudes toward, 66–68; Growth Era, 64–66; knowledge of, 80–82; post-revolutionary, 58–60

Poniatowska, Elena: *La Noche de Tlatelolco*, 72

popular classes, 14, 54, 88, 119n12, 121n4 (chap. 4), 122n3 (chap. 7); living standards of, 16, 98

population growth, 25; urbanization and, 26–27

Portales, Rosa (pseudonym), 50

poverty, 41

Prado, Manuela (pseudonym), 33–34, 36

PRD. *See* Partido de la Revolución Democrática

presidents: powers of, 58, 59

PRI. *See* Partido Revolucionario Institucional

privileged classes, 14, 116–17

professionals, 5, 44, 62, 80

public health sector, 39

Puebla, 62, 73

Puente, Laura de la (pseudonym), 44

race, 19

Ramirez, Patricia (pseudonym), 71

real estate, 53

rental properties, 50

Revolution, the, 94; goals of, 65–66; politics of, 58–59, 82

Reyes Heroles, Jesús, 10, 57

Robles, Susana (pseudonym), 34, 36

Rojas, Eduardo (pseudonym), 42, 44

Rojo Amanecer (film), 72

Rubio, Angela (pseudonym), 52

Ruíz, Marta (pseudonym), 50

Ruiz Massieu, José, 78

rural sector, 19, 23–24, 27

SALA. *See Statistical Abstract of Latin America*

Salazar, Jorge (pseudonym), 71

salesmen: traveling, 31–32

Salinas, Carlos, 21, 41; economic policies of, 77–79; middle class opinion of, 78–79

San Antonio, 31

San Ildefonso Preparatory School, 68

San Luis Potosí: free-text activists in, 62–63

savings, 39, 40, 54

schools, 5, 62, 64; private, 17, 30, 39, 40, 42, 48–50, 55, 99–100; public, 28, 31, 32

segregation, residential: of middle class, 19

skiing, 40

social capital, 45, 46, 51–55

social class, 12, 120n18; definitions of, 6, 10–11; and political culture, 80–82; survival strategies of, 54–55; trust and, 121n4 (chap. 6), 122n5 (chap. 6). *See also* class structure; occupation

social mobility, 20, 29–30, 93–94; examples of, 31–36

social trust, 82, 121n4 (chap. 6), 122n5 (chap. 6)

spending, 45. *See also* consumption

state-owned enterprises: privatization of, 38

Statistical Abstract of Latin America (SALA), 119n14; class structure analyses, 115–17

stock market, Mexican: collapse of, 40

strikes, 62, 69

students, university, 68–72; and 1968 student movement, 21, 72, 121n1 (chap. 5). *See also* Tlatelolco massacre

supermarkets, 19

survival strategies, 45–55; class differences in, 53–55

Taos (New Mexico): travel to, 40

tariffs: elimination of, 38

teachers, 5, 32, 40, 43, 44, 120n5

teenagers: in labor force, 51, 55

telephones: in home, 6, 16, 17(table), 96, 97(table), 116

Terminal de la Selva, 3

tertiary sector, 26, 120n2 (chap. 2)

Tijerino, Amalia (pseudonym), 34–35, 36, 40, 42, 43
Tijerino, Aurelio (pseudonym), 35, 36, 40, 42, 43, 50
Tijerino, Ricardo (pseudonym), 32, 36
Tijuana: Colosio's assassination in, 78
Tlatelolco: 1985 earthquake in, 75
Tlatelolco massacre, 21, 58, 68–74, 83, 94

UNAM. *See* Universidad Nacional Autónoma de México
unions, 59, 60
United States: middle-class migration to, 51
Universidad Nacional Autónoma de México (UNAM), 69, 71, 121n1 (chap. 5)
universities, 36, 39, 98, 121nn1–2 (chap. 5); protests at, 68, 69, 72; public vs. private, 5, 49–50
urbanization, 26–27

vacations, 5, 13, 39, 40, 47–48
Valdivia, Francisco (pseudonym), 52
Valdivia, Maria Elena (pseudonym), 52

Valle, Susana del (pseudonym), 51–52, 55–56
Vélez, Amalia (pseudonym). *See* Tijerino, Amalia
veterinary practice, 43, 56
Villanueva, Pedro Joaquin (pseudonym), 43
volunteers: in 1985 earthquake, 76
voting patterns: in presidential elections, 87–91, 102–4

wealth: accumulated, 17, 53, 54
Weber, Max, 11
white-collar jobs, 16, 27. *See also* occupation
women: as heads of households, 18; social mobility of, 33–36
workers: politics of, 60, 80
World Values Surveys, 107

Zapata, Emiliano, 59
Zapatista guerrilla movement, 78
Zedillo, Ernesto, 78, 86, 91, 120n2 (chap. 3)

ABOUT THE AUTHOR

Dennis Gilbert is professor of sociology and chair of the Department of Sociology at Hamilton College and holds a Ph.D. from Cornell University. He is the author of *La oligarquía peruana: historia de tres familias* (1982), *Sandinistas: The Party and the Revolution* (1989), and *The American Class Structure in an Age of Growing Inequality* (2003).